THE BLUE STONE
An Adventure in Spirituality

THE BLUE STONE

An Adventure in Spirituality

Karen Lavie

The Blue Stone, an Adventure in Spirituality

Copyright © 2022 by Karen Lavie

All rights reserved. No part of this publication may be reproduced or transmitted by any means, without prior permission of the publisher.

ISBN: 978-0-473-64198-6 (print)
ISBN: 978-0-473-64199-3 (ebook)

Published by Klarity Publishing

For Sebastian and Jacob,
who chose to be my sons this time round

UNFOLDINGS

Nicola's Foreword ix
We are invited to join a guided tour of Eternity

Time Travellers xiii
We are introduced to our fellow-travellers

The Space of Time 1
We learn that time is not what we think it is and get to know our tour guide

Navīd 11
We visit a community where people have forgotten who they are

The Garden of Plenty 33
We become acquainted with a wanderer who is on a desperate quest but doesn't know for what

The Birth of Baddar 59
We come to understand that seeking doesn't always mean that we will find

The Blue Stone 93
The path becomes clearer

Compassion speaks   119
We start to feel our common ground

Portals of the Heart   129
We are shown the way

The Sage   147
Red threads are unravelled

Epilogue   163
We hear how everyone lives happily ever after

Acknowledgements   169

About the Author   171

NICOLA'S FOREWORD

We are invited to join a guided tour of Eternity

For several years, I attended weekly classes in spirituality. There, I learnt about the nature of life through the wisdom of beings that no longer live on Earth. This was possible thanks to Ian, a medium.

Along with a few others, I would meet up with a group of spirits. Just like that. They told us about their 'lives' in that other realm, and we could ask them anything we wanted. It didn't take long for it to feel completely natural to have conversations in this manner – the beings we met were so very real, so recognisably human. They could be funny, outspoken too, and had no qualms about voicing the odd criticism of the way we do things in our part of the world in the twenty-first century – 'of course, we understand,' they usually added. Without exception, they saw themselves as souls in progress, which gradually helped me to understand that I was too. There was no need to be perfect! It was a crucial discovery, reassuring and liberating.

After I had been part of the Thursday group for quite some time, we were treated to something a bit different. It was a cycle of stories, featuring events from the lives of a group of souls whose destinies were intricately interwoven, as we were to discover. These stories contained elements that were more complex and far-reaching than what we had heard until then, and most of these pages consist of this material. Among many other things, they served as a vehicle for essential learning about life before and after death. Another recurring theme was the need to always listen to our heart and never to allow its subtle knowing to be overridden. I'll never forget their warning of 'Don't let others influence you!' – Ian's normally gentle voice would take on a quality of urgency. All of this culminated in something our teachers from Eternity called the Portals of the Heart, a teaching device, in their words. I will try to give you a taste of it. Perhaps you have heard about the Portals already. We also got some idea of the relationship between what might be called destiny and free will, and I came to understand that both have a place.

With time, we came to feel close to these souls who at various times had walked the Earth as people like ourselves. Their stories gave us a chance to marvel at the astonishing variety of life's manifestation, heart-wrenching or mind-blowing at times, and often of breath-taking beauty. All of this was presented by beings with an expansive view of a multiplicity of dimensions, who looked at life on Earth with refreshing humour and liberating casualness.

Much has happened since, and the encounters I was so fortunate to be part of have changed my life forever. For a long time, I have thought that some of the beings who came to speak to us on those evenings should have a wider platform. The depth and breadth of their understanding of the human journey were so immensely valuable to us that I can't help but feel that others too should have a chance to be encouraged and inspired by the wider vistas they conjured up for me and my fellow-travellers. Now that those Thursday evening sessions are a thing of the past and most of the people with whom I shared this adventure have gone their own way, I have decided that the time has come for me to dive into my notes and make a selection from all the stories and conversations Ian channelled for us. When I told Ian about it, he gave me access to the recordings of the sessions, which he had carefully stored and labelled, enabling me to render most of the stories and dialogues in the words of our spirit-friends. It is timeless wisdom, and chances are you too will find in it whatever you most need at your point in time.

TIME TRAVELLERS

We are introduced to our fellow-travellers

Lozeh, who specialises in Past-Present-and-Future Lives
Old Sharuz, who has just died
Navīd, who has a dream
His father, who is fearful
His mother, who hasn't survived his birth
Ardashir, a village healer
The Wanderer, who feels torn
His Host, who welcomes him warmly
The Host's wife, who serves him ginger tea
An Old Man with a twinkle in his eye
Sarwhar, who leads his followers on a quest
Nila, a midwife, who could have been his wife
Andisha, who is pregnant
Janan, her husband
Baddar, who is born
Ramesh, who cannot follow
The Seeker for Stones, who finds the
Most Magnificent Stone the Earth Could Ever Yield
The Master, who rejects it
Esin, who shows him the way
The Sage, who is kind

THE SPACE OF TIME

We learn that time is not what we think it is and get to know our tour guide

I am standing on a beach, one still, starry night. In the distance, I can make out a small cluster of rocks. They are out to sea, but rest on the same ground I am standing on. It's almost as if they are breathing, and it crosses my mind that, like me, they are alive. I become aware of a soft, glowing light and notice a small flame on each of the rocks.

I enter the water, the rocks and the flames, or maybe they enter me. And in the quiet of the night, I realise another being is there, someone who is very familiar. It is a child. The child is my soul. It has always been with me, each lifetime on Earth I have ever had, and it will be with me in all the lives that are still to come, and long after. I have no idea how I know all of that, but I do. The soul-child is here to remind me of my origin, of who I truly am: part of Consciousness. Like the sea, the rocks, and the flames. Like the ground that connects us all.

It was the evening I first met Lozeh. He had come to guide us in a meditation to feel Eternity inside of us and ourselves in Eternity. Lozeh is a spirit. He explained that he specialised in past-present-and-future lives and could pick up a future life as easily as one from the past. It had been his passion since the beginning of time, 'if ever there was such a thing,' he chuckled. 'Our lives are like a string of pearls,' he said, 'some with magnificent depth and lustre and others that are less spectacular, darker or duller, but beautiful and precious in their own quiet way.' Meeting Lozeh was nothing short of amazing. His enthusiasm was palpable, and his respect for us as fellow-travellers seeking to find who and what we are in the guise of different lives, in different centuries and in different lands, was touching and encouraging. He didn't explain about future and past and why it was all the same to him. What could he have said that we would have been able to grasp? But suddenly I felt time as a space inside of me.

I think it was because Lozeh bypassed my intellect that I experienced time as a space. He somehow felt like timelessness itself. I would almost say he embodied it, but, of course, a body was the one thing he didn't have. That's how real he was, though. To talk about these spirits, we need a different vocabulary and a different tense, too. We have present tense, past tense, future tense … but eternal tense? Or is it eternal sense? I haven't a clue. All I know is that on that evening I caught a glimpse of Eternity.

Back home after the session, I wanted to stay close to 'the ground that connects us all'. I sat on the soft blue and orange-red floor rug in my bedroom, slowly finding my way back to that marvellous, spacious, yet intimate place, and pondering my experience.

If time is a space, there is no before and no after, no forward and no backward, no past and no future. Everything simply is, a vast repertoire of possibilities that is always there, the 'now' we should be living in, as enlightened men and women keep telling us. Still, this 'now' was elusive, because, like most people, I spent much of my time thinking of the past or the future. Too often, I seemed to miss that all-important present moment, along with its presumably great potential. 'Life is what happens while you are making other plans.' I had seen it written on a plate in a teashop once, and it had jolted me – so much time wasted already. But when Lozeh took me by the hand that evening, I suddenly saw that 'now' wasn't the single instant I might be experiencing at any given moment. Rather, it was like a doorway leading to myriad possibilities, shaping endless realities, a place where all things could be found.

Later, another thought occurred to me: if it is true that all of life's phenomena are to be found in a space and there is no chronology, there must be a different kind of order, one which we can't perceive as such. Timelessness must be the key. We would often be told in our sessions that time doesn't exist, but nonetheless it is central to our earthly lives. I couldn't begin to imagine what life outside of time might be like, but meeting my soul-child on a dark shore that evening with Lozeh shed some light on the mystery of time, giving me a clue to its permeability.

As a child, I was a linear, logical thinker, just like my parents wanted, an orderly, responsible little girl, my hair tamed in two tidy, symmetrical plaits, and much of that neatness I had taken into adulthood. But when my friend Sonia introduced me to a group of people who met every Thursday night to converse with beings from another realm who were channelled by someone called Ian, I set off on a path that would lead me to discover a completely different kind of order. The two of us were sitting at my kitchen table having dinner when she first mentioned it – I had made an asparagus and spinach quiche that had turned out rather well. I was surprised and a bit sceptical. My only knowledge of this kind of thing came from movies that depicted séances – people sitting round a table, and one of them, in a spooky voice, calling up a spirit, usually a deceased relative of one of the people present. There might be the sound of a door slamming, or a candle would extinguish of its own accord. An innocent, amusing pastime at best. At worst, naïve superstition or even fraud.

'It has nothing to do with the ghost of your great-great-aunt or something like that,' Sonia said, correctly interpreting the disbelief on my face, as I was wondering how an intelligent, down-to-earth woman like her could spend her time on something like this. 'It has a much wider scope. It's about people ... I mean ... beings ... spirits ... call them what you will, who tell us about their various lifetimes or the times in between their earthly lives. There's no spookiness, they just talk, like you or I would tell something about our lives. Except that they have a larger perspective. It's quite incredible, totally out of this world in fact – but really! – how they show the connections between people or events. It has made me realise how much everything is interconnected. It's been life-changing, honestly. Also, no matter what it is we talk about, they have an uncanny sense of finding exactly the angle that is in some way relevant for everyone in the group. Some of them are ... very evolved, I suppose, and there is so much we can learn from them. Others are not and might be struggling, and from them we learn at least as much. You must come along, I'm sure you'll like it.'

I was intrigued. Sonia was a nurse at a medical practice not far from where I lived with Colin, my eight-year-old son. We had met a few months earlier at the local gym, after a Pilates class. She said something nice about my somewhat unruly red hair as I was undoing my ponytail and shaking it out. Sonia had short, blond hair and rectangular glasses with blue frames that looked striking against her soft features. We ended up going for a coffee and had become close in a short time. She was nearly ten years older than I and happy living by herself. She loved her work, was an active member of her tennis club and quite a good pianist. A few times a week, she dropped in on her way back from work for a quick dinner. I treasured her friendship and trusted that if she thought this might be something I would like, I probably should give it a go. My marriage had broken up a year earlier. For many years, most of the people I met had been colleagues of Fred, my ex-husband. It was time to do something new, find my own friends, and since Charles had come to live next-door, Colin was keen for me to go out. Charles was seventeen and, according to my son, the coolest babysitter ever. They would play table soccer and watch TV and make hot chocolate or popcorn.

'Just come along once or twice,' Sonia gently insisted, as she got up from the table and picked up her bag. 'There is no need for a long-term commitment, and you can take it at your own pace. I'll pick you up on Thursday at 7.30, okay?'

Ian turned out to be a well-adjusted, young-looking fifty-something with a greying ponytail, who had discovered his channelling talents some twenty years earlier. Several days a week he was a landscaper, planting copper beeches and lacecap hydrangeas in the gardens of people too busy to do it themselves, or advising them on water features made with river stones or bamboo. He could probably have left his landscaping business and made a living from his mediumship alone. Much later, when we had become friends, I asked him if he had ever considered this. It was a sunny autumn afternoon. We had taken a stroll to a park not far from where he lived, and he suggested we sit down on a bench along the white gravel path. It took him a moment to get comfortable, crossing his long legs in their well-worn, roomy jeans this way and that. Then he turned his gaze towards me, his friendly hazel eyes slightly narrowed, a habit that came from spending much of his time outdoors in bright sunlight. It made the little wrinkles etched in the corners of his eyes more noticeable, which I found endearing.

'I thought about it,' he said. 'My mediumship took off much faster than I expected, and it's true that part of me would like to take it further, even though I don't really know what I mean when I say that. Sometimes I think "I'm just an ordinary guy who likes growing things in the soil. Why me?", but at other times I find myself wondering if maybe there's more for me to discover about this role that's been thrust upon me. Who knows, we'll see. For now, it's good like this …' His voice trailed off, his attention caught by the flaming red and golden leaves of the liquid amber trees around us. His face lit up. 'Aren't they gorgeous?'

For a while we sat without speaking, captivated by the spectacle of the trees in the soft warmth of the late afternoon. It was Ian who broke the spell. He sighed, uncurled his legs and looked at me thoughtfully. 'Thank you,' he finally said, 'it's nice to be able to share these kinds of moments.' We sat in silence for a little longer, then he came back to my question. 'I think I'd like to keep doing my landscaping work for as long as I can. I love working in gardens, you see, especially with trees. Also, it's good to balance the higher spheres by digging into the earth, getting my hands dirty. The scent of the soil keeps me grounded. It's essential not to lose your earthiness when you do what I do. The beings that speak through me also speak to me, because, even though I'm a trance-channel, I'm fully conscious, as you know, and I hear what comes out of my mouth. I'm always mindful of the danger that I might interfere somehow or identify with the wisdom that comes through me – that I will think it's me who is this wise, you understand? I don't want to forget I am an instrument. It has happened to others in my position – their ego marched in through the backdoor after a while.' He laughed. 'You never know! It's better to have another, more ordinary job, to help keep things in perspective. Just in case.' I thought of a couple of infamous cases, but would never have put Ian in that category and told him so. 'Thank you,' he said, 'I appreciate your trust. I'd like to think I have enough awareness, but it's not easy, and my landscaping work really is a big help.'

I had never given that aspect of Ian's work any thought, but suddenly I saw how difficult it must be for people like him. They have to be so aware that what is said with their voice and vocabulary isn't what *they* said. Ian had to let go of any identification with Ian the Landscaper or Ian the Channel – with Ian full stop, in fact – in order to be a conduit for a Consciousness that was immeasurable, far beyond anything a normal person in a human body could grasp. The wisdom he shared with us every week was of a kind that could never come from just one man – or woman.

'There's another reason why I love my work with gardens so much,' he continued after a while. 'When I'm planting a tree, or designing a pond or a pergola, I can have some input myself, be creative, and that's something I need. I'm convinced that ultimately, no matter what, when you love what you do and can be present enough, Consciousness will express through you. It's always debatable if something is "my" creativity or the universe's, and I've come to see that there is no point in trying to distinguish between them, as they are really one and the same. Landscaping is like channeling in that sense: the more I can let things be, the better the outcome. I've been a landscaper all my life, and when I start a job I have lots of ideas – about textures and colours and borders and elevations, and whether to use natives or deciduous trees, or maybe go for a more exotic look. Those kinds of things. And that's all fine, of course. I love it when I'm given free rein and can do something just the way I like it. Still, I'm almost always aware of something else that's beyond me, and I know I get the best results if I go along with it. That's when I feel that I am in true partnership, that I'm co-creating with the universe. It's a kind of intelligent energy that comes from something much bigger than me, but at the same time is part of me. From what I gather from the beings I channel, this is the best way to do anything at all. We need to remember that we are Consciousness expressing itself, rather than Ian expressing himself or Nicola expressing herself. Do you understand what I mean?'

I knew exactly what he meant, although I had never thought of it in those terms. When I am experimenting with recipes for a new cookbook, I usually start with a plan, and then something takes over, an idea I didn't know I had – like that time I found myself adding brandy-soaked pieces of date to a basic chocolate cake mixture and then, as an afterthought, sprinkling pomegranate seeds on the satiny glazing, finishing it off with a few sprigs of mint. Just one mouthful whisked me away to somewhere warm and exotic, and I knew I was on to something.

This conversation with Ian marked a turning point for me. I learnt from him to consciously step aside at crucial moments. My body and mind are still involved, of course. Like Ian, I am not so completely absorbed that I don't know what I am doing. But this insight into the nature of co-creation turned out to be invaluable, in both my work and my personal life, and since then, whenever I feel truly inspired, I understand what is happening and allow the inspiration to take over.

When Sonia first told me about Ian, I googled the topic of mediums and was surprised at how many I could find online. Most of them appeared to be established and reputable, and at the same time normal, approachable people. Once I had met Ian, this didn't surprise me. It seems that channeling isn't such an unusual gift as perhaps it once was, and that more and more people are willing to make themselves available to be messengers of beings who could be very helpful and articulate, if only they had a mouth to speak or fingers to type.

THE SPACE OF TIME

My discovery of the Space of Time, as I came to think of it, happened my very first evening with the group. Some of the others commiserated that I had been thrown in at the deep end, but it couldn't have been a better start for me. The experience that time is not linear, or, at least, knowing that it doesn't need to be, was crucial for my understanding of what was to come. Also, I had felt a lightness that was to be a hallmark of all the conversations I would be part of. It helped me see that my problems and struggles were a normal part of life, and never random, and to treat them as such. Never did I feel an expectation to agree or conform. It all was very empowering. Soon, the Thursday meetings became the highlight of my week, and I formed friendships with Elspeth, Jason, Herman and some of the others.

The sessions were held in a small yoga studio behind John and Magda's house. Ian had designed their garden for them, and that was how they met. It was a Japanese-inspired courtyard, featuring small maples with delicate bright green and brownish-red foliage. A few weeping maples had been planted around an enormous white stone that looked like a pile of oversized pancakes. Sweet-scented, white-flowering creepers ran along the flagstone path to the studio. As soon as I entered the garden through the heavy wooden gate, I heard the water that trickled from a hollow tree trunk into a small pond with just enough room for one soft-pink waterlily and its large, heart-shaped leaves. In summer, we could hear the water through the open windows of the studio.

NAVĪD

*We visit a community where people
have forgotten who they are*

After only a few sessions, I felt completely at home with Ian and the others. It was as if I had discovered a missing link, and it was strangely reassuring to see myself in a much bigger context. It all made so much sense.

One particularly beautiful Thursday evening at the beginning of spring, I was early and spent a few minutes looking at a garden statue that Magda and John had recently bought. They had given it a place close to the mini-waterfall. It was a female Buddha with a child, sculpted in soft white stone. As I stared at her face, which expressed a fierce tenderness, I was taken back to the day I held my own son in my arms for the first time and experienced exactly the feelings I saw in that beautiful face. I would never have understood that expression before the day I gave birth to Colin – an intense sense of protectiveness, strength and vulnerability, all at once.

Magda had been watching me from a distance and slowly walked up to me. 'Do you like it?' she asked softly. When I nodded, my eyes still on the figure, she told me she had chosen it because it reminded her of her son and what she had learnt from him, simply by being his mother.

'I understand,' I said, 'I can feel that too.'

Magda's son was at university and had just moved out of his parents' home. It was no coincidence the statue had appeared now, I realised. Colin was eight. Our sons were no longer babies, but for each of us the statue struck a chord. When I looked up, I saw tears glistening in Magda's eyes. I linked arms with her, and together we walked into the studio.

'Hello everyone,' said Ian, looking around, 'I think we can start'.

He never took long to get into his trance. He would close his eyes, take a few breaths and then 'someone' began to speak. It looked deceptively straightforward.

'Good evening,' our visitor began, 'be welcome. I've been looking forward to this opportunity to talk to you again.'

Ian's pleasant, light voice didn't change much when he channelled. His delivery reflected in subtle ways the essence of the spirit-entities that talked through him, and we had a sense of them as beings distinct from Ian himself. Their energies seemed to be well-calibrated with his. It was easy to know who was speaking at any given time.

'I have a story for you,' our guest continued. 'You know by now that the stories we tell you on these Thursday evenings, as you call them in your time-bound reality, are peopled by an assortment of human beings and set in a wide array of places and eras. Even so, there is a red thread. Everything is connected. It is one of our main themes. We can see your desire to understand your life-journeys beyond what might be immediately obvious, and we are delighted if we can be of assistance. In all probability, you have heard that All is One and perhaps have wondered about it, as it often doesn't feel like that where you are. And of course, between life on Earth and the ultimate reality in which, indeed, All is One and divine in nature, there is as yet a rather big gap.' He laughed. 'Let the thought of Absolute Oneness inspire you if it does, but don't worry if it doesn't. All you need to concern yourselves with in the meantime is whatever happens to be there for you in the here and now, as it is the beginning of everything else and the most reliable indication for your next step. We know this is not always easy, mainly because of the human mind, which forever tries to persuade you to look ahead into an uncertain future, or to remind you of your frustrations, resentments and traumas of the past. However, rooting yourself in the present moment is the only way and a fast-track to enlightenment, in case that's what you are after. Ha-ha! There is no rush, I assure you. Take your time to smell the roses!'

Most of our guests used the pronouns 'we' and 'I' arbitrarily. They explained once that they didn't have personal identities anymore and had merged into groups. They might assume an identity for the sake of communicating with us, but frequently reverted to 'we', which was obviously more natural to them. It felt a bit incongruous at first, but I got used to it. It also served as a reminder that they didn't speak on behalf of themselves, but drew from a larger pool of knowledge and experience.

'Our stories are chosen to give you a peek at other souls who chose the human journey, just like you,' our guest carried on. 'We believe that meeting them will inspire you and reassure you that everything you experience has a place and a purpose. Please don't expect some big, amazing Purpose when I say that. Life has an inherent messiness, I am afraid to say, or, at least, that's how it almost certainly seems to you at times. It's about trusting that there is a purpose for every experience, rather than knowing what exactly that purpose might be – and being comfortable with that not-knowing. This is your challenge, in a nutshell.

'From where I am, I can enter any event in the Space of Time and see it unfold in front of me, a bit like you would watch a movie. The images and sounds are extraordinarily vivid. If you imagine a kind of ultra HD, three-dimensional screen with surround-sound, you might have an idea of how we perceive things here. I hope that, together, your medium and I can find words that will help you see the unusual happenings I'm about to describe and do justice to the strange beauty of the place and the curious beliefs of its people. Seen in terms of time as you experience it, this happened several thousand years ago, in a very old culture. The aspect we would like to highlight is the way these people saw "evil". We wouldn't blame you if you called their beliefs and rituals strange or primitive, but please keep in mind that your twenty-first century, civilised world is still far from clear on the nature of good and evil. Perhaps these events will give you something to contemplate. Enjoy the movie!'

I suddenly knew who was talking. All of our guests so far had moved through Time with great ease, but announcing a story about an ancient culture that practised rituals we might find primitive, while mentioning in the next breath our latest technology ... it could only be Lozeh, with his passionate interest in lives that span the far corners of Eternity. How wonderful to have a chance to meet him again. With a sense of pleasant anticipation, I let myself be taken along by the 'movie'. It had started ...

> ... the sun was just beginning to come over the top of the mountains to the east, but people were already gathering for the ceremony. Old Sharuz had died the previous day, and the rituals for the dead were held during the early hours of the morning, when it was still cool. The people wore long white or faded-pink robes, their heads and necks protected with scarves

against the sun. In the afternoon, no one would be about. They would all be resting in their huts made of pale-orange clay or having quiet conversations under the trees. After the ceremony, they would work in the terraced fields on the edge of the village where they grew their food – lentils mainly, and onions and carrots. A few men and boys would take a herd of goats further down the mountain to find some grazing.

Sharuz's body, covered with bark and leaves, was resting on a low mound of sand in the middle of the open space that was the community's meeting place. Behind it, just a short distance away, under a rooftop supported by dead tree trunks, the village elders were making preparations. To one side of the structure were some large trees that were held in high esteem by the villagers, because of the shade they so generously provided and the healing properties of their leaves. Other, smaller trees – figs and a few pear trees – were scattered in clusters among the dwellings. A little further along, in the shade of a large stand of walnut trees, some women were drawing water from a well. The mountain chain had kept the people who lived in this community in isolation for centuries. It took three days on foot on hazardous mountain paths to reach their closest neighbours, and rarely did anyone undertake the journey.

Even though they lived peacefully with one another, they had a curious belief in the power of evil. They were convinced it was inside their bodies, just like blood, inextricably part of them, and they lived in permanent fear of it. When they died, a ceremony was performed whereby the body was cut in several places to release the evil embedded in it. Only then were they free.

Sharuz was fifty-three and had enjoyed good health. It was his time, and he had known it. Rarely did people live much longer. His three sons with their wives and children were the first to arrive. They walked up to their father's body and waited there. Their mother had died a few years earlier. Soon, a large crowd had gathered to honour Sharuz and help expel the evil from him. They stood round the body in silence, close together. Two men who had been waiting with the elders started to softly beat a big drum. Once they found each other in a steady rhythm, one of the elders began chanting, a low, monotonous kind of melody. After a while, everyone joined in. They had been attending these ceremonies since they were small children and knew exactly what to do. The drumming and chanting slowly induced them to gently rock back and forth to the rhythm. Gradually, the chanting grew louder and their heads started shaking and their feet stamping, the unrelenting beat echoing in their bodies, reminding them of the evil within each of them until their turn to leave the physical plane. As the rhythm accelerated, a man moved forward and stood in front of Sharuz. When the music reached its high point, he raised a wooden dagger up in the air and plunged it three times into Sharuz's body. The chanting stopped abruptly, but the drumming continued, slowly growing fainter. When the drum too was silent, everyone stood quietly, until the beat in their bodies had faded. Then they walked away to begin their day, except for those whose task it was to burn the body.

Navīd was seventeen, slender and good-natured, with curious dark eyes. He liked the strong sense of togetherness when they were chanting, and feeling the drum reverberating in his body. Rather than reminding him of evil things, it gave him a sense they were all one big body. As he slowly walked away from the village square, still under the spell of the ceremony, a strange thought entered his mind: if they all had evil within them, why did it never show itself? There were occasional fights and disagreements between people in the village, but surely that was not evil? And they were always quickly resolved, sometimes with the help of the elders. No one seemed to bear a serious grudge against anyone else, and people were always prepared to help each other. Where or what was this evil? Did they really carry it within them? All of them? Sharuz had always been so kind, sitting in front of his hut in the evening when the sun had gone down, greeting him cheerfully when he walked past. It was hard to imagine there could have been evil in Sharuz.

The thought stayed with him for most of the day, and that night he had a dream. It was unlike any dream he had ever had – he wasn't asleep, but he wasn't awake either – and in that state, he felt himself being taken somewhere that was both far away and close by. There, he was shown a world that was very different from the one in which he had grown up – a world where people lived in the secure knowledge that they were divine beings and inherently good. He knew without a shred of doubt that this was the true nature of humankind, and that there was no such thing as evil except in people's fearful minds. In the morning, he woke up remembering every detail and felt relieved of a great burden. Life would never be the same.

He couldn't wait to tell his father. His mother had died when she gave birth to him, her first child, and he and his father had always been very close. Even so, his father stared at him in undisguised horror as Navīd told him about the dream and his realisation that there was no evil inside people or any need to cut open their bodies after they die. The father had brought up his son with the traditional beliefs of their community and knew that he had never had any opportunity to be in touch with other ideas. He could only conclude that his son must be out of his mind.

'Stop!' he shouted, 'do you hear me? Stop! I want to hear no more of it.' His face had turned red, and he was breathing heavily. 'You have no idea what you are talking about, no idea whatsoever! Come with me. We'll go and see Ardashir straight away.'

Ardashir was the village healer, a small man with pale-green eyes. Upon hearing about Navīd's dream, he confirmed the father's fears that something was seriously wrong with his son. He told him that the evil in Navīd had become so big as to possess him, and he immediately started preparing for a long healing session to exorcise the excess of evil. As he couldn't use the ceremonial knife that freed the dead from the evil in their bodies – we would like to reassure you of that! – he carefully selected some dried herbs, which he kept in a basket in a corner of his hut. Then he went outside to gather twigs, rocks, sand and bits of plants, ingredients to help anchor Navīd to the land and the beliefs of his people. When Ardashir came back, he spent a long time breaking, crumbling, mashing, sifting and combining them, and then he sprinkled the mixture over Navīd, who was lying on a bed of sand and bark on the ground, all the while reciting sacred words to bring him back to the consciousness of his tribe. After this, he arranged rocks in a circle round Navīd and started the complex ritual for exorcising an excess of evil, which involved all kinds of spells and incantations and lasted for most of the day. After about eight hours, Navīd woke from a deep sleep.

'Navīd?' Ardashir asked softly. 'Navīd? Are you all right? How are you feeling?'

Navīd blinked against the light for a while and sighed deeply, before slowly turning his gaze towards the healer.

'Yes, Ardashir,' he finally said, 'I'm fine. I feel much more grounded, I think, and calm and settled. It's amazing what you have done. Thank you, thank you so much.'

Ardashir was exhausted after the long session, for most of

which he had been in a trance, but he smiled when he heard this. He had always liked Navīd and his father, and he was pleased that he had been able to help them.

'You can get up now and go home,' he said. 'Take it easy for a while!'

The moon was full that evening, and very large, as if you would only need to stretch out your arm to touch it. The villagers were sitting in front of their huts, enjoying the cool air and admiring the pale light of the giant moon. Navīd too was outside, together with his father, sitting a little along from his aunts and uncles and cousins. They were leaning against the clay wall of their hut, which still radiated warmth from the intense heat of the sun. He felt deeply peaceful after the treatment he had received from Ardashir, and was in awe of the wondrous moon and the way it lit up the huts and the trees and the faces of the people. He became conscious of his father's voice, asking him if he had recovered from the session with Ardashir.

'Yes, Father, yes, I have, thank you.' He was quiet for some time, but then he spoke again. 'I feel relaxed, and there is a wonderful clarity in my head. You know, after Ardashir's treatment, I'm even more convinced that evil doesn't exist. Look around you, Father, look at the people enjoying that gorgeous moon. Look at the children, how wide-eyed they are, how mesmerised by that magical light. How could there be evil in any of them? There is no evil, Father, I'm sure of it, please believe me. Ardashir's work has somehow deepened the experience I had in my dream. It was a true experience, Father, much more than just a dream. Do you understand? It was the truth. I know it was, because I can still feel it resonating in my body, the same way I felt the drumming yesterday at Sharuz's ceremony. Only stronger. Much, much stronger.'

When his father heard this, he became very frightened. His son must have lost his sanity completely, if even Ardashir couldn't make him see differently. He spoke quietly but urgently. 'Son, you are a danger to the community and to yourself with these kinds of ideas. I can't let you walk around like this. I want you to go inside now and stay there for thirty days. Don't speak with anyone. Contemplate, until you see the truth: that we all have much evil inside of us. Is that clear?'

Young people in that society had deep respect for their elders. Navīd nodded, looking wistfully at the scene around him, trying to soak up enough light and beauty to last him for thirty days. Then he got up and followed his father inside. He shed many tears in those thirty days, tears of boredom and loneliness and of longing to be outside in the company of his friends and family. After thirty days, in which nobody said a word to him, not even the aunt who prepared his meals, his father called him, invited him to sit down with him in a corner of their hut, and spoke to him for the first time.

'This is the thirtieth day,' he said. 'How are you, how has it been for you?'

Navīd looked at his father, an expression of relief all over his face. 'Thank you, Father, thank you! I'm so happy that you are talking to me again! To tell you the truth, I didn't find it easy to be alone for all that time, and there were moments when I thought I couldn't bear it any longer. But, as you see, it hasn't done me any harm in the end. I'm fine, I really am.'

His father looked at him suspiciously. 'Don't tell me again that you feel even more sure of what you saw in your dream.'

'No, no, on the contrary, Father. This time by myself has given me much clarity, and I see now that what seemed a true experience was in fact the fruit of my imagination. Or maybe it was wishful thinking, I'm not sure, but true it was not. Thank you, Father, for giving me the opportunity to see my mistake. Of course it's true what you have taught me since I was little, that we all carry evil within us. I don't know what came over me, but I can see it clearly now.'

The father was delighted that he had saved his son.

A few days later, he observed Navīd guiding some goats back up the mountain, a faint smile on his lips. The smile was barely noticeable, but it unsettled him. As soon as there was no one else around, he took the opportunity to talk to him.

'You look very happy, Son.'

'Oh yes, Father, I am,' Navīd replied. 'I'm so glad to be back with you and the others. I missed it. I didn't like being on my own. I am thankful that I can be outside again and have people to talk to.'

'I promise I shall not punish you, Son, but I need to know the truth. Did you renounce your dream only because you wanted me to let you come back with us?'

'Father, you know the answer!' Navīd said with a broad smile. 'Yes, it's true that I told you what I knew you wanted to hear, but I didn't think that I should be punished for having a dream. Don't worry, though, I won't speak about it with anyone.'

The father was furious that his son had lied to him. It was unheard of that a young person would speak in such a way to an older relative, especially a father. At the same time, it was out of character for Navīd, who had always been respectful. The father deliberated. If he punished his son, he too would not be true to his word, and he couldn't do that. So he said nothing.

But something had changed. Navīd was more at peace with himself than anyone else in the village. Their language had no words to express 'being at peace with oneself', but people noticed it all the same, and they started to seek him out. In his presence they too felt more inner peace. He never spoke about it. He was just one of them, sharing the work and attending the ceremonies for those who passed away.

One day, about five years later, Navīd was walking back from the fields with his cousins, when his father took him aside.

'Navīd, do you remember when you lied to me so that I would let you go outside again?'

'Yes, Father, of course I do.'

'We've been sharing everything all these years since then, Son, and I must say that it's good to be with you. It was always good between us, needless to say, but there has been something different about you, ever since that day. I'm sure you know what I mean. Was it that dream or hallucination you had the night after Sharuz's death? I've been telling myself that I should enjoy your company without asking questions, but I've come to a point where I want to understand why you have been so different since that day.'

Navīd looked his father in the eyes, then stared ahead of him, his brow furrowed. He was completely still for quite some time. Then his face relaxed and he spoke. 'Father, would you like me to tell you the truth, or shall I lie again?'

His father was taken aback when he heard this. He hesitated for a moment. 'Um, as a matter of fact, I'd rather you don't say anything at all, because suddenly I am afraid of what your answer might be.'

'That's fine, Father, I understand.'

But his father couldn't leave it alone. Nearly every day for five years he had wondered why his son was so different. When Navīd left the hut later that afternoon he followed him, catching up with him a little further along the path to the well.

'Son, it's no good pretending. I have to know.'

Navīd suppressed a smile. He slowly nodded. 'All right, Father, yes, you are right, it's time I told you. But we'd better sit down somewhere. What I'm going to say might be a bit of a shock, and I wouldn't want your heart to stop beating all of a sudden and have to watch as they pierce you with a knife to release your evil.' He laughed softly and pointed at a walnut tree nearby. Its widespread branches were close to the ground, creating a shelter. 'Let's sit over there. There's no one around, it's a good spot.'

As they made their way to the tree, the father raked his beard with his sweaty hands, wishing he had never asked, but he knew there was no way back. With a pounding heart, he lowered himself under the tree.

'Explain to me, Son,' he said in a small voice, once they had made themselves comfortable. 'What is it that you haven't told me? I have to know, even though part of me would rather not. Do you understand?'

'Yes, yes, I do, I understand it very well,' Navīd said quietly. Then he started. 'Father, I told you five years ago about an experience I had in a dream; how I was shown a world where people were unaffected by evil, and how I instantly knew this is our real state of being. Their actions can be evil, but people themselves are never bad. If they commit evil deeds, it's because they are afraid, Father. There's a big, dangerous world out there, or, at least, that's how it often seems, and it makes them feel small and insignificant. Often, they are overwhelmed by life's relentless challenges – finding water, protecting themselves from the elements, defending their lands and crops against invaders … They fear for their security, for their own lives and the lives of their loved ones. People are vulnerable, and life can be daunting. But that's all it is, Father, fear. My dream reminded me that we all come from a source of pure goodness. We are divine beings, and deep down everyone knows this. It's just that most of us have forgotten.

'You, Father, you know this too. You know it intimately. There was much more in my dream than I told you at the time. I didn't think you would be able to take it, because you reacted so strongly to what I said, and I was afraid you might feel you had no other option than to kill me, or yourself, or even both of us. But now that you have asked me, I believe it's the right time to tell you about our connection as it was laid before me in my dream.' He stopped and smiled encouragingly at his father, who was hunched with fear. 'Don't be so worried, Father, it will be all right, really, please trust me.' He hoped his father would be able to listen to what he had to say.

'Maybe I should tell you first that it wasn't a normal dream. It was as if I was taken away from my body so I could see everything from a different perspective, a bit like when you stand on the top of a mountain. And from there, I saw that the life we are living now is one of many, and that our souls keep wanting to be born again. Each time, we experience ourselves in a different way and acquire a deeper understanding of who and what we are. We always want to learn more about the nature of the universe and our place in it. In my dream, or vision perhaps, I saw that, in another life, I was your father and you were my son. In that life, you had a dream very much like mine that showed you that evil doesn't exist. Like me, you were immediately convinced of its truth, but, not long after, you started to doubt it. What you had been shown seemed preposterous, and you were afraid of what the consequences might be if you even so much as breathed a word of it to anyone. We lived here, in this same village, where people had believed for centuries that human beings consist in large part of evil, just like they still do today. You wondered whether to talk to me, to your father, but in the end you decided to be prudent and pretend it hadn't happened. Never did you speak about it with anyone, and towards the end of your life it had become a faint memory. You lived until you were nearly sixty years old, and after you died they stabbed you three times. No evil was released, because there wasn't any, and as you were observing your own ceremony – you know, Father, how the soul often hovers around the body for a little while after death – you remembered the dream in all its detail. And instantly it made sense to you, and you felt great sadness that you hadn't been able to accept this vital truth about humankind and to tell others about it. You suddenly knew that, more than anything else, that was what you had wanted to do.

'Much later, when it was time for you to start making plans for another life on Earth, you wondered how to experience again, in one way or another, the truth that all people are of divine origin and evil is only an idea in people's minds, but you weren't sure if you would have the courage to see it through. You thought about it at length. Our souls have all the time in the world, Father, and take great care with the planning of a life. You spoke with guides and others in Spirit, and also with me, who had been your father, and together we thought of a way for you to learn what you wanted to learn, one where we would work together, you and I. The plan was that we would change roles. This time, you would be the father and I would be your son. My mother, who contributed to the plan as well, volunteered to return to Spirit after my birth, so that you and I would have more opportunity to develop the strong bond we would need. As a young adult, I would have the dream instead of you, and then share my experience. Like this, you could hear about it indirectly, in a way that might feel safer. What would happen afterwards was left open. It would depend on your confidence and trust and also on how patient and compassionate I could be. Because, in spite of all the planning in between our lives, Father, once we're here we act from our free will. Outcomes aren't set in stone.

'So far, everything has happened the way we planned it. My dream, quite naturally, frightened you enormously. All you could think of was taking me to Ardashir. Ardashir is a great healer, with a strong connection to his divine Source, and all he did with his spells and herbs was reinforce the truth of what I had just learnt: that evil doesn't exist. He provided me with the support I needed. It was the only thing he could do, for he too was part of the plan. But, of course, he had no idea of it.'

Navīd stopped talking. His father shuddered and covered his eyes with his hands. This was outrageous. Had his son been mad all this time and somehow managed to deceive him? For a while he fought with his emotions – anger, confusion and plain fear. But then he looked at Navīd, whose eyes reflected deep understanding and quiet certainty, and suddenly he remembered. And as he remembered, he knew beyond any doubt that what his son had just told him was true. He had felt the oppressive weight of the evil that was supposed to be inside of him lifetime after lifetime, and he had longed to get rid of it. A moment later the memory was gone, but he was left with the realisation that his son, far from being mad, was in touch with a source of wisdom he himself was far from.

They sat in silence under the tree. The hottest part of the day was over and a cool breeze played around their faces. Navīd saw tears welling up in his father's eyes. Gently, he put a hand on his father's shoulder, and so they sat, without speaking, for a long time.

Finally, the father said: 'I love you, Son.'

Navīd nodded, full of concern for his father. It was dark when father and son at last got up to make their way home, their path lit by twinkling stars.

The next morning they got up and started their day as they had done all their lives. The father seemed to have recovered from the surprise, but in truth he was in great turmoil. Later that day he called Navīd into their hut. 'Navīd, come here, please, I have to talk to you.'

'Yes, Father, what is it?'

'I've been thinking all night about what happened between us yesterday. I can't deny that you gave me an experience of a kind I didn't know existed. Maybe one day I will thank you for it, but right now I can't. It's strange and extreme, and it makes me very uncomfortable. I can't have you around me any longer. It's not right. I have to ask you to leave. If all that you told me is true, we might meet again, and if it's not ... then so be it.'

Navīd sighed and nodded, bravely forcing a sad smile. He had known all along there was a chance this would happen. 'If you want me to go, Father, then I will,' was all he said. He packed a few belongings and enough food and water to last him the three days it would take him to reach the outside world. His pack slung over his shoulder, he stood in the doorway. His father sat on the floor in a corner, hugging his legs tightly, his forehead resting on his knees. Navīd waited, hoping to see his father's face one last time. 'Good-bye, Father,' he finally said, but his father didn't look up. Navīd lingered a moment, then stepped through the doorway and began walking up the path towards the mountain pass.

It was the end of the day, and people were coming out of their huts to fetch water and make preparations for the evening meal. When he came to the end of the village, he turned to look at the land, the trees, the dwellings and the meeting place of the community where he had lived all his life. His eyes went towards the hut where he had left his father huddled in a corner, and he drew in a long breath. He stood there for a long time. After a while, he began to notice people were watching him intently. As he felt their eyes on him, he was acutely aware of their complete integrity as human beings, and they in turn had a moment's recognition of their divine origin. He knew that a seed had been planted. 'One day, they will see the truth, which, in their hearts, they already know: that there is no evil within any of them.'

He turned towards the mountains and left.

We sat in silence for a long time after Navīd had gone. It was indeed like being in the cinema – after the closing credits, when your thoughts are still with what you have just seen and you don't feel like leaving your seat yet. I was touched by Navīd, by the wisdom of someone so young, by his unswerving trust in what he had learnt in his dream and by the way he had treated his father – with so much loving understanding. In spite of all that, I couldn't help being perturbed by the … casualness, almost, with which he had mentioned that his mother hadn't survived his birth as 'part of the plan'. I thought of the intense joy Colin had given me, the warmth of his little body against mine as he was drinking, his first wobbly steps, first endearing baby-words – being so intimately part of the life of another being as he was gradually coming into his own. Would I have known what I had missed if I hadn't survived his birth? I felt deeply for the mother of Navīd, who hadn't seen her son grow up to be a wonderful human being.

'Are there any questions?' Lozeh finally asked, shaking me out of my thoughts.

'Yes,' said Jason. 'I'm wondering if it could really happen that someone has ideas that are so radically different from those of the society they grow up in. Is it at all possible? In reality, I mean?'

Lozeh laughed. 'The stories we tell you are real. There is no need for us to invent them, because we can choose from all the stories humans collectively create in the course of living their lives, and so there is a never-ending supply. We understand what you mean, though. Usually, young humans indeed adopt the ideas and beliefs of their elders, particularly in conditions where communication with people who might think differently is limited. We realise this rarely is the case in your world, with its teenage rebellion and all the information young people have access to via technology. That the story of Navīd and his father took place somewhere that was very isolated by anyone's standards was no coincidence. It was impossible for Navīd to have got this insight from anywhere else than Consciousness directly, and it's true that something of that nature doesn't happen very often. He was a soul with a mission, and as he explained to his father, the events had been carefully planned. It was, however, a huge step for the soul who was his father in that life, and for many others in their village, to be exposed to a fundamental truth that went against everything they believed. Navīd was motivated by nothing but love – he had no personal agenda whatsoever – and he wanted to help his people to make a decisive change in their belief system so that they could live their lives with more lightness and freedom.'

When Lozeh said 'lightness and freedom' I suddenly had a sense of what it might be like to go around convinced there is an evil substance inside of me. It felt depressing. What sort of relationship would you have with yourself if you felt like that all the time? Would you despise yourself? Feel permanently guilty? How would you be able to live with yourself, let alone love yourself? I sighed and was grateful to live in a time and place where indeed there was more lightness and freedom. Then the thought struck me that in our society self-acceptance still was a difficult issue. We might not think there were malicious particles circulating in our bloodstream, and psychologists seemed to agree that anything that could be called evil originated in early childhood experiences, but, as Lozeh had mentioned at the start, how much further advanced than the people in Navīd's village were we really in this respect?

'Thank you,' I heard Jason say. 'If I may ask one more thing, please? You mentioned Consciousness just now. I don't suppose you could give us a kind of definition? I had a sense of it, when you said that Navīd had this insight from Consciousness directly, but could you say a bit more about it? I have often wondered.'

'We aren't very good with definitions,' said Lozeh – a wide grin appeared on Ian's face. 'We find them a bit limiting, most particularly for Consciousness, which, as you might have heard, is infinite and all-encompassing. We could say to you that it is massive and formless and fuelled with divine intent, but that would raise more questions than it answered, wouldn't it? However, when you said that you had a sense of it, you were actually quite close. Even though each of you would be hard-pressed to explain what Consciousness is, you all have a sense of it, an indefinable, common sense. All of you are conscious, and you know it. Consciousness has nothing to show for itself, if you forgive me for putting it like that. It's like a torch that illuminates whatever you shine it on. In fact, you could see yourselves as torches, shedding light on all kinds of things, simply by being who you are. We try to inspire you to point your torches in certain directions, so that it's easier to find your way.'

I thought of the meditation on my first evening with the group. I had experienced myself as Consciousness then and had not felt the slightest need to make sense of it. It had been spontaneous and completely natural. It was reassuring that it was clearly possible to experience something as profoundly true, even if it couldn't be defined or explained. This realisation itself was enlightening, and I was thankful to Lozeh for pointing my torch.

'Excuse me?' came John's voice after a little while. 'Is it all right to ask another question?' Ian nodded. 'Would you be able to talk a bit more about Good and Evil? I really appreciate this idea of our innate divinity and all that, but still, it feels a bit idealistic to me, or naïve perhaps. I mean, it's hard to deny, isn't it, that there are people out there who are downright evil? I'm thinking of some of the cases I've seen pass through the courts, for example.'

John was a judge of many years. I imagined he would have come across a great many terrible deeds. What was wonderful about our group was the variety of our backgrounds and experience, and each of us was drawn to different aspects of the story. For me, it was the fate of Navīd's mother. Jason, as a dedicated high school teacher, was always wondering about the inner world of young people. For John, it would inevitably be the issue of evil itself.

'Yes, of course, that is a legitimate question indeed, especially coming from a judge.' Lozeh laughed and paused for a moment, but then he became serious. 'The answer was given in the story,' he continued, 'when Navīd explained to his father that even though people do what he called evil deeds, these are induced by fear of one kind or another. Naturally, as a society, you have to concern yourselves with these. Humankind as a whole is still rather far from a sense of Oneness, and in the meantime you need to have something in place that protects you from the evil deeds of others, from their crimes, as you would say. It's unavoidable for now, and that's why you have your justice systems. We do not feel that justice is always done through those systems – please don't take this personally – but we are in agreement with you that, mostly, it cannot be different, at least not at this stage of human evolution. In the end, however, it is just as Navīd said, and whenever we look at an individual soul who does something that is harmful in whatever way, we invariably find a deep sense of insecurity or fear. There will almost always be feelings of not belonging, or inferiority, of not being loved.

'All these have their roots in humanity's core issue of separation, your sense of being separate from Divine Consciousness – some of you might prefer the word Source, which illustrates that it was the beginning of everything. For the longest part of Eternity, Consciousness was completely at one with itself and creatively exploring its nature. It was a playful approach; ideas were simply tried for a while and then discarded. But then the notion of selfhood arose, and it set in motion a sequence of thoughts that eventually caused pockets of Consciousness to feel like separate entities – you must know that thought has hugely creative power. This was the beginning of individuality.

'It was also the start of duality – with the awareness of self, naturally there had to be non-self. "Self" provided a perspective to perceive what was outside of itself. You can understand that you need some distance for that – to separate out a bit. Being in the world in this way makes for compelling experiences. You all know that, of course – creating realities is your favourite pastime, after all.' Our narrator paused for a moment, but not long enough for any of us to question this intriguing statement. A smile crossed Ian's face as our guest continued his explanation of duality. 'Once a sense of self-and-other was firmly established, people began thinking in terms of opposites that they took to be mutually exclusive. From "self or other" came "right or wrong", "good or evil", "black or white", to name just a few. However, as Consciousness is an indivisible whole, which is another way of saying that All is One, real separation is impossible. Can you see that? It was just an idea! This is why you might have heard it said that separation is an illusion. It was unavoidable that duality would arise in this process, and it couldn't have been different. In order to create and have experiences as human beings, you need to feel the pull of opposite forces. This is also why nothing is ever stable for very long in physical reality, and you regularly experience crises of some sort or another.

'We know this is a rather complex topic and that it is difficult for most people to accept that evil is ultimately not evil. Without a doubt, this will come up again in our conversations. For now, it would be good if you could believe us that everything and everyone is an inextricable part of Consciousness, and that an undivided whole cannot be two opposite things, even though, from your perspective, the world seems to be full of those.'

THE GARDEN OF PLENTY

We become acquainted with a wanderer who is on a desperate quest but doesn't know for what

It was nearly two years after we had heard about Navīd. We had many guests during that time, different kinds of souls. Some were in the middle of their reincarnation cycle and told us about their most recent lives or the logistics of planning their next life. I gradually gained insight into the reasons for souls' coming into physical bodies. We almost always come with some kind of life issue in the form of a belief that blocks us from recognising our own and others' divine nature, a false belief therefore, also simply called a block. Life then steers us towards particular circumstances which reflect that belief. No matter our understanding of our blocks when we are in Spirit, we can only really learn through experience, and it appears that the School of Physical Reality on Planet Earth is the best place for this. Through our spirit-friends, we were shown many examples of the ways in which humanity's beliefs are played out, and I began to get some idea of just how large the universe is. Infinite, as they said, a concept I never managed to get my head around completely. I came to understand that infinity isn't a borderless space forever stretching into more space – something I could never conjure up without sooner or later bumping into the end of it – but, rather, the endless creative potential that is inherent in even the most fleeting of thoughts anywhere in the universe; each of these thoughts then projects many other thought-like vibrations, and so on and so forth, multiplying … indeed *ad infinitum*. Any of these have the potential to become manifest – what most people consider 'real' – depending on the circumstances. I started to appreciate that there were facets of the universe that would never meet or even know of one another's existence, even though all were part of the Oneness. A few times, we heard from souls who had never embarked upon physical reality. Apparently, coming to planet Earth as a human being is one of many options available, and we learnt that for those who choose to express through a human body, which, obviously, was a choice we ourselves had made, there is complete freedom as to how, when, where and with whom to undertake the journey.

This particular evening turned out to be the beginning of a kind of series, as I came to think of it, but we didn't know that at the start. The spirit who spoke to us was a guide. Everyone on Earth has a spirit-guide, I had learnt, often more than one. Ian closed his eyes, and as I was drawn into the silence I felt my everyday little worries subsiding. As always, it didn't take long for the guest of the day to find his way to us.

'Greetings to you all,' he started. 'I am honoured to be here with you. Like all of you here, without exception, I had many lives in a physical body. I enjoyed most of them and suffered in a few others, but I can tell you in all honesty that I remember that period of my soul-development with fondness. No other kind of existence allows you to experience such singular focus and intensity. Enjoy it while you can! I no longer return to Earth, and spend most of my time (so to speak) guiding others. The last time I was on Earth was several thousand years ago. I can hear someone wondering how it can be that I relate so easily to you and converse in contemporary language. Consciousness is whole, as we have told you. There are no barriers of any kind. We can pick up quickly on new developments, be it Google or shopping malls or ADD, and even the possible connections between them. There is nothing wrong with any of those, don't worry! They are simply learning tools, of which every period in history has a few. We choose a certain time and culture to incarnate, because external circumstances play a role in whatever it is that we are to learn and experience, but once you are back here, in Spirit, time is no longer relevant. Where I am now, there is no time, only being. Time is incompatible with being. This is because time is a concept, whereas being is a reality. A concept evaporates in the presence of what is real, of what is. It functions as a kind of crutch, until you are close enough to see the reality behind it. Then you can throw the crutch away or give it to someone who still needs it. So you could say that time doesn't exist, but that's not how it is for you. Timelessness is something you will experience when the time is right, ha-ha. I'd better get on with what I came for.

'I speak to you tonight as the personal guide of an ambitious, courageous soul who is very dear to me. I have been his guide on several occasions. These kinds of bonds are strong. As guides, we have a profound understanding of the souls we are guiding, both of their deepest desires and of the fears and beliefs that stand in their way. Of their temperaments and emotions too. He and I are very alike, and I once had an experience much like his. You'll understand when you have heard the story.

In this life, he is a wanderer. He has been travelling for a long time, ever since he left his parents when he was sixteen years old. That was when he felt a deep need to discover what else there was in the world, apart from the village where he had lived all his life with his parents and siblings. He had a strong sense that there was something more, something completely different and profoundly meaningful, and he simply had to find what it was. His mother cried when he announced he wanted to leave, but both his parents understood his desire and gave him their blessing.

Many years went by and he did not return to his village. Occasionally, he stayed in communities, helping in whatever way he could. Sometimes, this was because he needed a rest. Other times, he was attracted to the people who lived there and wanted to spend time with them and get to know their way of life. The longest he ever stayed in one place was a year, because he had fallen in love. The girl was beautiful and intelligent, and whenever he told her about his adventures, she was spellbound. He loved her more than he had ever loved anyone, but in the end he couldn't face committing to her for the rest of his life and relinquishing anything else that might come his way. One moonlit night, with a heavy heart, he quietly left the community and his bride-to-be. Once he was on his way again, the pain of leaving his beloved abated, and he knew he had taken the right decision.

For years he wandered, discovering new places, meeting different people and learning a variety of skills and languages. He liked being under way and loved the changing landscape and chance meetings that were part of it. Even so, a thought gradually took hold that perhaps he should find a place to finally settle. Without a doubt, there was still much more to see and learn and experience, but he was starting to feel weary. Slowly, he came to realise that, beneath the surface, people and places were much more alike than he would have thought all those years ago when, young and energetic, he set out to find something more meaningful than what life had shown him until then. He started to wonder if what he was seeking really existed. If it did, surely he would have found at least a sign of it after all this time?

This is his frame of mind when we catch up with him, a tall man with thinning, shoulder-length hair and inquisitive green eyes, carrying very little. The frayed sleeves of a woollen undergarment are just visible under his threadbare tunic, and he wears loose-fitting trousers that once must have been white. The straps of his leather sandals are tied round his ankles. He is past his prime but looks strong and vigorous. He goes round a sharp bend in the path and sees a little below him, sheltered by high mountains on three sides, a glorious valley. He stops to take it all in. What a magnificent sight, after all those days of walking along grey, monotonous mountain paths, seeing only the odd goat nibbling at a shrub or a bit of tough grass. The valley is unlike any he has ever seen, wide enough to receive the sun for a large part of the day. It is bordered by two mountain streams, and a smaller stream cuts across it. No wonder it is so green. Curious and elated, he follows the path downhill. His slightly troubling thoughts have lifted. Even his vision seems clearer, but maybe that's because of the purity of the air. He smiles at his own exhilaration as he strides down the widening path. When he gets to the stream, he notices a man on the other side. Someone who lives here probably – he looks fresh and rested and is not carrying anything. The man has seen the traveller's approach and indicates a place in the stream where it is easy to cross. Once the Wanderer joins him on the opposite bank, the other greets him cordially.

'Peace be to you, stranger, be welcome! You must have come a long way. I live just a little upstream from here. Would you like to join me and my family for a meal?'

He is of average height and looks fit and healthy. He is wearing a brownish-red woollen jacket, and it crosses the Wanderer's mind that it must be wonderful to have such a garment. The gentle, friendly demeanour of the local man warms his heart, and when their eyes briefly meet in greeting, he feels the other's genuine interest. He gratefully accepts the invitation. As they walk into the valley, he is awe-struck. There are gardens and orchards with all kinds of vegetables and fruits – apples and apricots that look plump and sweet, nut trees, almond too. A little further on, radishes are growing and other vegetables he doesn't know. In the distance, he recognises barley with golden stems, nearly ready to harvest. Along the paths, there are flowers of every imaginable colour. Everything looks gorgeous and healthy – what a wholesome, harmonious corner of the Earth!

The meal, a few hours later, with the man and his wife and their three children – a girl of about ten, who is the spitting image of her mother, and two playful younger boys – is wholesome too: a variety of vegetables cooked in a fragrant yellow sauce, with goat's cheese and a kind of grain that is chewy with a slightly nutty flavour. It has been a very long time since he ate so well, and he thanks his hostess profusely. After they have eaten, they all rest for a while on the soft grass next to the house, which is roomy and much more comfortable than any dwelling he has seen in years, and then his host offers to show him around. The Wanderer follows him curiously. Wherever he looks, he sees this is a place of unusual prosperity. It is immediately obvious that the people who live here do not have the kinds of stresses many others do. Their faces are relaxed and open, without the signs of worry or anxiety he has often encountered on his travels. He is introduced to men and women who are chatting in little groups and working in the gardens. He sees them picking fruit, pulling out weeds here and there, and watering the soil with the clear water from the stream.

Some of the children are helping to collect the water in small wooden containers, splashing it around and having fun. Older children play with younger ones or carry babies and toddlers. A little group is engrossed in building a structure of stones and sand and bits of foliage, pouring water into tunnels from which it flows into little ponds. A couple of boys are trying to find a way to contain the water in the ponds. Others are chasing one another and rolling around in the grass. In a meadow a little further on, children are making chains of little bell-shaped flowers, which they hang round each other's necks. The Wanderer stays behind to observe them from a distance, thinking how wonderful it must be for children to grow up like this – how freely they move their bodies, how creative they are and how inclusive of one another.

He starts walking towards his host, noticing in passing the ripeness of the fruit, the clarity of the water and the friendliness and camaraderie of the people with whom he exchanges pleasantries, but he is also conscious of a kind of restlessness, irritation almost. He decides to ignore it as best he can. It is too beautiful here to be troubled by unsettling thoughts, but he is unnerved all the same. He catches up with his host, who has stopped to help pick some apples.

'What a beautiful place this is!' he says. 'I watched the children play and talked with a few people, and everyone is so friendly and relaxed. I have travelled for most of my life and met with many wonderful people, but never have I seen a community quite like this. It's truly extraordinary what you have here.'

His host is pleased that his visitor is so appreciative. He knows that this is an unusual place, and he is proud of it. 'I don't know what your plans are,' he says after a while, 'but if you like, you are very welcome to stay here. We easily have room for more people.'

The Wanderer remembers that, earlier that day, he wondered if maybe he had seen all there was to see and it was time to settle. The face of the girl he once loved appears in front of him – he hasn't thought of her in years – and suddenly he is aware of a desire to share his life with a woman. For a moment, he is overwhelmed by his contradictory feelings. It would be wonderful in so many ways to live here, but the restlessness he felt earlier was real.

'Thank you! Thank you so much,' he finally says. 'Thank you for the offer. I … I'm not sure what to say, to tell you the truth. Could I think about it?'

'Of course,' the other replies. 'You must be tired. Stay with us for a few days and give it some time.'

The Wanderer thanks him again and together they walk back to the house.

He sleeps deeply that night. It has been a long time since he had a soft bed on which to stretch out his body. When he wakes up, the house is silent. Quietly, he gets up and goes outside. The first rays of the sun are stroking the mountaintops. It is still cool, but he can tell it will be a beautiful day. He walks over to a narrow stream that runs close to the house, and stands there for a while, noticing other, similar houses and thinking once again what a magnificent place this is. He slowly squats down to scoop up some water with his hands, and splashes it over his face. He gasps for air, and his breath quickens. How wonderful to be alive!

He decides to follow the stream for a bit and starts walking away from the house. There seems to be no one about, and, apart from the soft murmur of the water and the clattering sound of

THE GARDEN OF PLENTY

the odd pebble skittering away from his feet, there is silence. After some time, he spots a flat piece of rock, perfect to sit on, overlooking a meadow covered in dew. The sun has fully risen over the eastern ridges now, and for a long while he is mesmerised by the glistening dewdrops stretching ahead of him. He looks in wonder at the jagged, snow-capped mountain peaks that almost surround the valley, their outlines sharp against the intense blue of the sky. There is a sudden splash, and when he directs his gaze back to the stream he notices a quick movement of red and yellow – a couple of fish darting past. It crosses his mind they are there to impress him, that they want him to appreciate the abundance of this place in all its colourful detail. It makes him smile. The invitation to stay is at the forefront of his mind, and as he breathes in the pure mountain air he feels tempted to accept. And yet, there is that other feeling, that there is something out there of a different order from what he has known so far, different from even this valley. He sits on the rock for a long time, trying to understand himself, contemplating what all of this could possibly be about, but his ambivalence stays. Finally he gets up and starts walking back.

When he gets to the house, his host and the children are nowhere to be seen, but his hostess is there, and she welcomes him with a smile. He can't help noticing how well the deep-yellow of her soft-woollen tunic suits the olive tone of her beautiful face, and for a second time in less than two days he thinks how wonderful it would be to have a woman in his life. She offers him a large cup of ginger tea and a slice of still-warm barley bread dripping with golden honey. As he thanks her, her dark eyes seem to size him up, and suddenly he is struck by the thought that, somehow, she knows what he is going through. It is a feeling he has never had before, and he finds himself wondering about it for a while after.

Towards the end of the day, his host takes him for a walk towards the far end of the valley. They stroll in companionable silence, and the Wanderer is conscious of the serenity of his host – so different from his own disquiet as he mulls over the choice he is faced with. Finally, he breaks the silence.

'Excuse me, do you mind … um… could I ask you something?'

'Sure.'

'Everything you show me here is just amazing. It's a miracle that life has led me here, to this beautiful place. I hope you won't misunderstand me when I ask you this, but I can't help wondering if … I mean, would you please tell me … is there anything else here?'

His host is astounded. 'What do you mean "Is there anything else here?" You have seen how blessed our life is, that we live in harmony and good health, that our children are growing up to be responsible, well-balanced human beings, that our Gods provide for us generously. What else could we possibly want?'

The Wanderer hastens to say again how much he admires and appreciates everything he has seen, but that he really would like to know – and here he struggles to express what he feels – if maybe there is something utterly, completely different, something of another order, perhaps. His companion looks confused and shrugs his shoulders.

'I've no idea what you are talking about. There is nothing other than this. It's all I can show you. I'm sorry if it's not enough for you.'

The Wanderer apologises, afraid that he has offended his host. He realises the latter thinks fundamentally differently to him, but he can't help feeling that something is missing here, and it's impossible for him to imagine how anyone could be truly fulfilled without it. During his many years of solitary travel, he has, however, learnt to look at himself with a degree of objectivity, and he remembers how he felt just before the valley came into view. For a brief moment, he doubts the existence of 'something completely different and profoundly meaningful', which he has been seeking ever since he was young. Could it be that his host is right, that this is all there is? They continue walking alongside the stream without speaking, except to point out a particularly lovely tree or a little side-stream cutting through a meadow. When the sun dips behind the mountains and the first stars appear, he is entranced, and for some time all thought of what might make life truly meaningful disappears. However, as they approach the house, in spite of himself almost, he addresses his host one more time.

'I'm sorry, please excuse me for being insistent. It must come across as disrespectful perhaps, but my questions concern something I have been pondering for almost as long as I can remember. It has nothing to do with you or this beautiful valley. Please know that I tremendously admire the wonderful way in which the people in your community live here together, and I very much appreciate your invitation to stay. It's just that … could I ask you something personal?' The other nods, wondering what is on the mind of his unusual guest. 'When you come home after you have worked in the fields and gardens … and you eat with your family and play with your children … and then later, when you have kissed your wife and you lay your head on your pillow … what do you dream of? What is it that you dream of, that you have not yet attained?'

The other blinks in total surprise. 'I don't dream of anything other than what I have. I thank the Gods. I thank my wife. And I thank others in my life.'

The Wanderer starts to feel a bit agitated at this point. He makes an effort to smile, nods his head as if understanding, and thanks his host for answering such a strange question. In spite of that brief moment when the thought crossed his mind that what he has been seeking all his life may not exist, he cannot believe that the other man doesn't have a dream. He doesn't want to appear impolite by pushing the point any further and is glad when they reach the house.

During his travels, he has witnessed first-hand the kinds of quarrels and disagreements that seem to be inevitable when people live together. He decides to look out for these kinds of things in this community. Everything in this valley simply seems too good to be true, and it makes him edgy. For several days, he observes the children at play and the adults at work. Harmony prevails, the sun shines, crops continue to be gathered, and everyone seems genuinely happy and helpful and considerate.

A few days later, he is alone with his host once again. They are sitting on the grass next to the stream he discovered on his first morning. It is after the midday meal, which he very much enjoyed, with its many interesting flavours, most of which he had never tasted before. As with all the meals he has shared since his arrival in the valley, it was eaten in agreeable near-silence, and now, too, there is little conversation between him and his host. He is weighing up whether to ask him one last time if he really doesn't have a dream and if the complete harmony here is enough to give life meaning. He listens to the burble of the water – never before entering the valley was he so conscious of the sound of water and how soothing it is – and asks himself if he really wants to discuss the matter again. Wouldn't it be better to simply enjoy this idyllic spot and try to relax? He knows, however, that he must get to the bottom of what is troubling him, and this is a good opportunity. He watches his host, who is trailing his hand in the water while dreamily staring at the mountains in the distance. If only he could be that serene. It takes him a while to find a way to start.

'Is it all right if I talk to you for a bit?' His host nods, almost absentmindedly. The Wanderer takes a deep breath, then continues. 'I've been here for four days now and have watched the grace of life in your valley. I have seen the exquisite quality of what you grow and how healthy and happy you all are. Ever since you first asked me, I have been seriously considering staying, but the truth is I feel torn. It's hard for me to believe that there isn't a dream of some kind deeply buried inside of you. Are you absolutely sure?'

His host looks at him indulgently. By now, he has become somewhat used to this stranger's allusions to dreams and visions and other ideas that are rather foreign to him. Slowly, he takes his hand out of the water and turns towards his guest.

'I am sure,' he says in a low voice, smiling gently. 'I have no such dream. I have all that I desire. I have health, I have a wife and children who I love with all my heart, and they love me. I have friends. The climate is perfect. We have delicious food and more pure, fresh water than I could ever wish for. I have everything anyone could possibly want. What more could I dream of?'

'So, there isn't anything, anything at all, that you desire, which your life does not afford you? Not even when you are in bed, in the quiet of the night? Something whispering in your ear that there might be more than this and you just don't know it?'

'No, my friend, no. How many times do I need to tell you? I have all I could possibly wish for and so does everyone else here. I'm simply grateful and that's all there is to it.'

The Wanderer is quiet. A strange sadness creeps over him. There is something about his host and his wife and most of the other people he has met that is very appealing and feels right somehow, but he knows he has to leave this valley.

When he finally speaks again, it is with some difficulty. 'As much as I would love to stay here, and, believe me, there is a part of me that really would, I never could. This could never be enough for me. I don't blame you if you don't understand it, because I hardly understand it myself.'

At this point, it is his host who has a question. It has gradually become clear to him that his guest is experiencing some kind of crisis, and he wishes he could help him. He leans forward. 'What is it, then, that you hold as a dream?' he asks softly. 'What is it that you are looking for, which you cannot find here with us?'

The Wanderer is moved by his host's concern, but he has no idea of his own inner motives. All he knows is that it is impossible for him to stop searching.

There is a long silence.

'Bless you, and thank you for your hospitality,' he finally manages to say. 'I understand why you ask this, but I don't know what it is. The urge I feel to continue is simply too strong. I will leave early tomorrow morning.'

The next morning, his host supplies him with food and water. To the Wanderer's delight, he presents him with a jacket like his own, except that it is dark green. 'It goes well with your eyes,' he mumbles with a shy smile, 'and you will need something warm.' The Wanderer is deeply touched, and wonders if he is making a mistake. He quickly shakes off this doubt, however, and thanks his host for the generous gift and for all he has done for him. They embrace, and he takes the path towards the mountain range, in the opposite direction from where he has come.

When he is some way into the foothills, he stops to look back at the valley. He can see the neat rows of crops and the children scampering about and the blue wood smoke curling into the crisp, clean air. It is paradise. As he follows the rock-strewn path, the hills become a wind-swept mountainside. The contrast with the lushness of the valley couldn't be greater. Yet, he is compelled to continue.

There is no sign of human life until, at the end of the afternoon, he notices someone coming towards him. Naturally, they stop and greet each other. The other is an older man, almost too old to be walking in these mountains, you would say. He is a little bent over and supports himself with a bare, solid-looking branch. His silver-grey beard is rather untidy. He is wrapped in a big brown woollen shawl and his bright blue eyes twinkle. The Wanderer takes an immediate liking to him.

'Hello, traveller,' the old man says, 'what is it that brings you to these parts? This is a rather desolate, uninviting place, cold and uncomfortable. Why would you want to take this road?'

The Wanderer is glad to have someone to talk to. 'I guess you are right, it isn't very welcoming here, even less than I expected. I didn't particularly plan on coming this way. I suppose I took this road on an impulse. You see, I have been wandering for most of my life. As long as I can remember, I've had the feeling there must be much more to life than what's visible on the surface, and I left my family in order to discover what it is that I could be missing. I have stayed in all kinds of communities. It has been insightful and often heart-warming to experience so many different people – the diversity of their beliefs and the ingenious ways in which they organise their communities and give their lives meaning. The last few days, I have experienced something so unlike anything I had ever seen before that it has left me with much to think about. It was when I entered the valley just below here. You will pass it on your way. It's a most wonderful place, where everything is plentiful, and the people live in complete harmony and peace. But I felt agitated and had a distinct feeling that there is a dream these people aren't dreaming, if you know what I mean. Living in harmony and being happy and healthy seem to be all they want. I had been considering finally settling somewhere, and this would have been a good place, but when I realised that the people were completely fulfilled, I felt that I must continue and find out what my dream is. I have a strong sense that it must exist, although in what form I don't know.'

Something about the old man makes the Wanderer ask if he knows what that dream could be. The other looks at him kindly, but slightly mischievously at the same time.

'Yes, I do indeed. You are going up the hill and I am going down. I wish you well and bless you on your way.'

'Please don't go yet!' says the Wanderer. 'You know my dream? Really? Do you think you could possibly …?'

'If you are sure you want to keep going,' he says, 'you will make a discovery, and then you will be clear about this dream of yours.' This leaves the Wanderer a little confused. How could this old man know such a thing? Before he can ask anything else, the other has carried on down the path, calling a friendly goodbye over his shoulder.

The Wanderer continues, climbing higher into the mountains. It dawns on him that he is not very well prepared for this adventure. He has not got much food, and the terrain is becoming difficult. There is no sign of life. Even the mountain goats, which kept him company in the beginning, steer clear of these heights. Yet something is urging him on.

At last, he comes to a kind of plateau. As nightfall is imminent, he decides to sleep there. While he is tossing and turning, trying to get comfortable, he seriously wonders if he could be mad. He walked away from the most beautiful place he has ever seen, inhabited by the friendliest people he could imagine. He left all of that behind because of a hunch, a mere idea, that there must be something better and loftier and he must find it. And now, because of that strange compulsion, he finds himself lying on bare rocks. It has become cold, and he is wearing all the clothing he was carrying, but even his new green jacket isn't sufficient to keep him warm. Finally, he falls asleep, overcome by doubt and exhaustion.

When he wakes up in the morning he feels refreshed, in spite of his dark thoughts during the night. He still has little idea of what it is that he is hoping to find, but he is convinced that he is doing what he needs to do. He suddenly becomes aware that he has company. It is the same old man.

'And? Do you know yet what it is that you are looking for?', the old man asks.

'To tell you the truth, no, I don't. Yet, when I woke up, I knew I would carry on and that it would be all right. I cannot answer your question, but this is what I must do.'

The old man, still with a twinkle in his eye, nods and wishes him well. The Wanderer is suddenly in a hurry to leave. He mutters a farewell and, without another look, goes on his way.

The path becomes steeper and narrower, and then disappears altogether. The terrain becomes more impassable by the hour. When night descends, he lies down under an overhanging rock on a ridge. There isn't much room and he knows he will not get much sleep. When he wakes early the next morning, he is aware of an inner voice: 'You must be a madman to come to this place,' it says. Another voice replies: 'Not at all, this is the right thing to do.' He feels his energy growing, even though, in reality, his circumstances are becoming more dire. But he keeps going, moving higher into the mountains, until, towards the later part of the day, the old man appears for a third time. He is friendly and courteous as before, but somehow sterner.

'Good afternoon! I have come one last time to challenge you. Where are you going and why? Why are you climbing higher and higher into these forbidding mountains, where there isn't even a flat place to lie your body at night, where there is no food and even water is hard to come by?'

This time the Wanderer answers without thinking. 'I don't know what it is that brings me here. However, there has to be something far greater than the sweetness of the lives of the people in the valley. There has to be something far more potent, far more powerful. There must be a way of being on this Earth which lifts us from mere existence, be it harmonious or not. I don't know what it is, but my instincts tell me to keep going, no matter how cold and lonely it is up here.'

The old man, still with a twinkle in his eye, says to him: 'Thank you for your truthful answer. I wish you all the best and will step out of your journey at this point in time. You must do what you feel you need to do.'

And he disappears.

The Wanderer continues climbing. The voice that says 'Are you a madman?' has become faint. The other voice is loud and clear: 'I don't know why, and I don't know where it will take me, but this feels right.'

He notices a shimmering on the horizon. As he is carefully stepping onto the next rock, he realises it is the highest point of the mountain range, the ultimate peak, glistening white and pure in the last sun of the day. He feels in every cell of his body that all that matters is that he take himself there.

Ian was quiet. Surely, it wouldn't finish here? Would he reach the pinnacle? And most of all, what was this mysterious dream he had? What on earth could be worth more to him than what he had found in that perfect valley? We waited and wondered.

After a while, the guide spoke again. 'I am sorry, but this is the end of the story. I know you are disappointed. Maybe you would like me to explain it a little?' We wanted that very much indeed, and after a brief moment he continued. 'You can probably see that this is a kind of archetypal story. It has all the ingredients: the eternal quest for a Holy Grail, and a Garden of Eden where people are simply happy and don't ask questions. Then there is an old man, complete with a twinkle in his eye, who appears out of nowhere and gives the protagonist the proverbial three chances to reflect and reconsider. You might have guessed that it wasn't an ordinary old man. It was me, his spirit-guide. We had agreed when he was planning his life that I would appear at a critical time to give him a chance to remember what it was he really wanted to find.'

He said no more, and in the ensuing silence I found myself nervously trying to think of a question, just so he would continue talking and not end the session at this point. I could see this was a classic kind of story, but I was puzzled by it. Fortunately, Herman came to the rescue. He had been one of the first people to join the group, several years before I did, a serious, softly spoken, but sharp academic. He had a real knack of asking questions that cut to the core of the matter.

'If you say an archetypal story, does that mean it's just a kind of fable? Or is this something that really happened?'

'As we mentioned on another occasion, ultimately, there is no difference. Everything that happens in each of your lives is what you might call a story. Some spiritual teachers in your time speak of "the movie that is your life", and that is quite a good metaphor. But to answer your question: yes, this is a life of someone I know very well and, as such, a true story. It is also true that I took some licence to embellish it a little here and there, but, essentially, this is what happened. You would be surprised at how often people live archetypal lives, particularly earlier in their reincarnation cycle. The feeling of "there must be something more or bigger or better" is at the heart of the human condition. The relentless, underlying sense of missing something that is both vital and elusive is an inevitable consequence of feeling separate from Source. It causes people to believe that no matter what they do or who they are, it's never enough. All issues that souls take into a human life are ultimately based on a perception of lack. It can be expressed as lack of money or health or friends, or of talent, fame and good looks. Or it could be a soulmate that is longed for, or a higher purpose that could make life meaningful. The list is long, and there are many variations on the theme. The underlying issue of almost everyone is lack of self-love, of which the other lacks are symptoms. Of course, there is no conscious memory of Source, and people who see themselves as seekers have no idea that there's no need to go on long, eventful journeys to find what they are missing so badly. They often traverse half the world, only to come back empty-handed. Your literature is full of stories of that kind, and so are the lives of my friend the Wanderer.

'The people in the valley lived with deep gratitude. The closeness within their community was not based on fear, as happens so often. Their togetherness wasn't inspired by a common enemy or a religion that excluded non-believers. They were so seamlessly in touch with their inner being that there was no need for them to think of themselves as spiritual in any way. They were intelligent and their language was rich and expressive, but they had no philosophy of life. They knew intuitively that too much thought divides, that it creates distance from the heart. They were rooted in being. The Wanderer had partial recognition of all of this – we see this in his attempts at self-inquiry, his repeated questioning of his host, and his genuine distress when finally conceding that he really cannot stay – but his dawning awareness was not yet strong enough, and he would need several more experiences to understand that everything he felt lacking was in fact right there. It's particularly poignant, because the ill-fated trek into those mountains is put alongside something that is simply perfect. The discrepancy between the valley with its life-affirming qualities and the stern, cold mountain range that didn't sustain any form of life couldn't have been larger. Even so, he found a way to attribute lack, and that's how it often goes. When the Wanderer finally recognised this for what it was, many lives later, he could see that nothing had been missing all along.'

I hadn't understood that this was what the story was about. That the right thing for the protagonist would have been to recognise the life of the people in the valley for what it was: divinity expressed as a slice of heaven on Earth. I guessed a few people in our group had identified with him and admired the fact that he wouldn't merely settle for an easy life, but instead was determined to 'follow his dream'. Wasn't that a strong theme in our culture? I had secretly imagined myself living happily in such a beautiful place, but had seen it as a lesser option and assumed I must be lacking the Wanderer's courage and depth.

Ralph was the first to stir. 'Excuse me ... um ... if you don't mind ... I would like to know ... you said "ill-fated". Does that mean that he didn't get to the pinnacle?'

The guide gently shook Ian's head. 'Did you think he did? When you see in your mind's eye the surroundings there? I think you know that it's wishful thinking that anyone, particularly someone so ill-prepared for such a trip, would make it to the top. This couldn't possibly end well. No matter how magnificent those mountain peaks might have been in the eyes of the Wanderer, there was no life. There was only the glistening of the pinnacle. Glistening is an exterior quality, something alluring, but once you are there – if it were possible to get there, for a start – there is no warmth, no heart, no sustenance, no company. And what's worse, once you've reached the pinnacle, you no longer can see it glistening in the distance, which is its only quality, and then there is nothing higher to dream of. Imagine the feeling when you realise that. Where could you go from there?'

'Could I ask something, please?' said Carolyn.

Ian's head nodded. 'Sure, please go ahead.'

'Why didn't you warn him more explicitly? He was so close to recognition. You could have made him give up, or, at least, told him that what he was looking for was based on a false belief. Couldn't you have done that?'

Carolyn was a lawyer at a firm in town and had joined our group a little while ago with some apprehension but a lot of sincere curiosity as well. She was an old friend of Herman's, and he had encouraged her and brought her along. She was in her fifties, a senior partner, and a thoughtful, good-looking woman, dressed in perfectly fitting jeans and delicate wool sweaters in reds and greens that suited her shiny, henna-dyed hair. Similar colours, I suddenly realised, to the jackets of the Wanderer and his host. How funny that even on this kind of level the stories matched our experience. It made sense that Carolyn was the one to ask this, but I was wondering about it, too. The man in the story had been so close to the 'right' choice which might have saved his life and contributed to the resolution of a significant flaw in his belief system. Why not give him a bit of help? For a moment, I pictured the scene in a courtroom. Imagine you have an agreement with someone that you will guide them, and then, at some critical point, you decide to leave them to it, resulting in a fatal accident – and then you are as off-hand about it as the old man was. It was easy to empathise with the reflex of a legal mind.

'I certainly tried!' our guest laughed. 'There were many clues he could have picked up on. When we first met and he asked if I knew what it was that he was looking for, I told him "You are going up the hill and I am going down." If he would have paid attention to those words, it should have made him think again. The fact that I came from the opposite direction suggests that I had made the same journey, but he didn't wonder what that might mean. He was too busy with his dream. He never noticed there was something about me. I gave him three chances to remember what the point of this whole exercise was, but he was incapable of seeing another perspective.

'Ideally, he would have stayed in that valley a bit longer. There was a woman there, in fact ... but four days were not enough for a meeting to take place, even though she was right there picking apples that first day, when his host showed him around. Mind you, he wasn't in a state of mind for that kind of thing. Even though once or twice he had a fleeting thought that he might like to share his life with a woman, this desire was overlaid by his preoccupation with a higher purpose. For most of the time, his thinking mind was obscuring his feelings. The only times he was fully present were when he observed the children absorbed in their play and when he felt a brief connection with his hostess, which was significant, by the way. For the rest of the time, he was distracted and not able to actually see the people and be open to what they could have shown him. That was a pity, but that kind of thing can easily happen. When he decided to leave, he could have returned the same way he had come, via the path that connected the valley with the rest of the world and was used by other travellers to and from the valley. There was no need to choose the mountain range, which was impenetrable, except perhaps with a very experienced mountain guide. That was why I stepped in, to see if there really was no other way than to let him go on. Even though in many ways he was an evolved soul, he suffered from a blind-spot. This is always caused by a strong belief that has been with us during most of our soul history. It blocks the light that could make us see a larger truth. Resolving those kinds of blocks is crucial on the way to enlightenment.

'In the story, I challenged him. In the end, I could see that the desire to find a higher purpose and the disdain for what he perceived as mere existence were still too deep-seated. Guides are respectful of an individual's decisions, and you mustn't forget there is always free will. The fact that he at least considered staying in the valley shows the belief was starting to shift. I understood it so well, because I too had carried this same idea with me for a number of lives. It wasn't difficult to accept his decision in the end. Ultimately, there is very little we can learn from the experiences of others. It's true that often the path can be sweeter and shorter, but many believe that the harder path must be the better one. I would like to take this opportunity to tell you that this is not the way it works. The idea of "no pain, no gain" contains no truth whatsoever. Going off into these mountains was plan B, if you like. Eventually, learning does take place and, with that, liberation from the belief that gave rise to the need for the life-lesson in the first place. A guide is there for support and encouragement, not to save others from learning.'

'Excuse me?' it was Elspeth. She was always scribbling away in her notebook, a serious student of spirituality. We had become firm friends and would often go for walks on the beach or for a coffee round the corner from where she lived, where we would discuss our Thursday evening gatherings. 'Could I ask something, please?'

'Sure,' said our guest, 'what is it that you would like to know?'

'That woman ... you mentioned that there was a woman in the valley whom he might have met? I'm wondering ... what would it have meant for her, the fact that he didn't even notice her, whereas, maybe ...' Her face had turned red as she was speaking.

'Are you asking if she was unhappy about not meeting him?'

'I'm not sure what it is that I'm asking exactly, it's just that I find it upsetting somehow – I mean, if she was right there?'

'We understand, of course. It would have been a wonderful thing to happen, wouldn't it, a kind of happy ending. This possibility was just one of many, though, and at a conscious level this woman had no idea of any of this. She hadn't been waiting for him nor was she missing him when he was gone. In all probability, she married someone in that community at some point and was happy enough. For my friend the Wanderer, it's true that it would have been a breakthrough, but the later events show us that he wasn't quite ready for such a solution. You always take contingency plans with you into a life. And because no one remembers the original plan anyway, there is no disappointment when you go with your contingency plan. Only once you are back in Spirit, you know again.'

Elspeth nodded vaguely, but something was obviously troubling her. She was sitting on one leg, and she held herself very still. There was a pensive look in her eyes, and the pen she had been taking notes with was frozen in mid-air. I suspected that the story had reminded her of the husband she had divorced several years earlier. They had a good life and a lovely house which they spent years doing up together. As in the story, their children were healthy and intelligent, and all that she wanted was for them to be there for each other as a family, and have friendships and an occasional holiday. Her husband, however, had been like the Wanderer, always striving for something better, forever looking at ways to expand his physiotherapy practice, even though it was successful and provided well for them. Holidays had certainly never been on his agenda. I wondered if Elspeth saw her husband as the man with a vision and herself as the unambitious woman who just wanted to be happy. He had always looked for more, and somehow had made her feel that she was less for being content with her life. It had been a hard lesson, but one she was slowly beginning to re-emerge from with renewed confidence in herself and her priorities in life.

Ralph coughed and tried once more. 'Sorry, but I'd like to get this straight. Are you saying that he didn't find what he was looking for? Not at all? Was it all for nothing? Or did he realise, before he ... before he died?'

'He had many experiences in that life and gained meaningful insights. He was capable of looking at himself and was open to the ideas of others. It was certainly not for nothing. A life never is, as the goal is exploration, and explore he undoubtedly did. It's true that he didn't manage to see past his block, but it was a very fundamental block, of a kind that often needs lifetimes of chipping away at. When he was back in Spirit, he was upset with himself at first, but his guides and others encouraged him and pointed out his progress. His mother was there to welcome him, along with one of his brothers. There were others, too, with whom he had relationships in other lives. Often, reconnecting with those souls carries a high level of excitement – the surprise of meeting long-lost friends and family members you had forgotten you had. Can you imagine? You recognise them immediately, memories of how close you used to be and how much you loved them are flooding in, and you simply carry on from where you left off. All of this helped him see his experiences in a different light and regard them with humility. He knew he would have to take this lesson again in some form or another, but in the meantime he was happy to be home.'

THE BIRTH OF BADDAR

We come to understand that seeking doesn't always mean that we will find

The following Thursday I was looking forward to what the evening would bring, but the Wanderer and his host still felt close, and I had a suspicion that I wasn't the only one who would have liked to stay in the valley a bit longer. It had been a true story, after all, and I had become fond of that magical place. As this was going through my mind, others were arriving, and I greeted them absentmindedly. Only when Ian came in and sat down did I put those thoughts aside. He looked around, gave us a friendly hello and closed his eyes.

After a little while, a being made itself known. It was a slightly different kind of presence than we had experienced so far. Even though personalities are shed on returning to Spirit, each of the spirit-people who came to see us seemed to have their own style. This one felt particularly inviting and drew us in at once. Ian smiled warmly as he accommodated its energy in his body, then started to speak.

'Good evening to you all! It's truly special to be here! I was invited by a soul you already know, and I was glad to accept. He asked me to tell you my story, which is also his story. It is a prequel, if we stick with the movie metaphor, to the story you heard not long ago, about the man who wandered off into the mountains, in search of something he thought was missing in his life.'

I was surprised and excited. It seemed that we could indeed spend some more time with the Wanderer and maybe some of the others too. I hoped he would fare better this time. But it was a prequel, an earlier life – assuming that our visitor was using words that conformed to our sense of time. Did that mean that he would be even more ambitious? I was terribly curious and urged myself to contain my thoughts and pay attention as that would surely be the best way to find out.

'Our story features quite a large group of people,' our guest continued, 'but he and I are the main characters – at least, from the angle we would like to share with you tonight. The reason we put the spotlight on the two of us is that we want to show you an example of reciprocal life-lessons. Often in our earthly lives we unwittingly facilitate each other's learning by mutually triggering certain thoughts and behaviours that are based on beliefs that are inconsistent with the truth of the universe, and therefore cause conflict. When such a belief is played out in front of you, you have a chance to see it and make adjustments. This will gradually influence your experience of life, because, as I think you know, your beliefs create your reality, not the other way round.

'It is generous of my friend and co-star to let me be the one to speak to you. He could have chosen to do it himself and present what happened from his perspective, whereas my viewpoint was an altogether different one. Much has happened since, however, and even though in the life I will tell you about we disagreed on a fundamental level, from the vantage point we have now we know we needed each other on that occasion. We had prepared the scenario as much as we could when planning our lives. You must keep in mind that in spite of our actions and opposing views, at a soul-level we are always motivated by love, and there is an enormous desire to help one another, no matter what it takes.

'For me, these events marked the beginning of a crucial insight, which showed me the way for many lives to come. I was a woman, and it is as a woman that I am speaking to you tonight. A soul is androgynous, or you could say that we have no gender, but when we speak to you we present ourselves as man or woman, so that it's easier for you to relate to us. My name in that life was Nila. My ally – let's call him that – whom you have already met as the Wanderer in the Garden of Plenty, was called Sarwhar. Here's our story.

There were about forty of us, men, women and some children. We had been walking for a long time, and we had no idea where we were headed or when and where this journey would end. Each of us had chosen to follow our leader, Sarwhar, whom we all loved and respected. We were on a quest to find Great Unity. In other times and other cultures, including yours, people might call it Truth or Awakening or God … it doesn't matter, words go out of fashion all the time. So, in our terms, we were looking for Great Unity, and we trusted Sarwhar to help us find it.

We had been travelling for years. It was unusual to walk for so long, even in that place and time in history, when it was not uncommon for people to cover long distances on foot. For us, however, it was a way of life. We would get water and other supplies from the settlements we passed along the way, and every now and again we spent some time in a bigger community so we could rest. Sometimes, some of the group members would decide to stay there and settle. It also happened that people from those communities joined us. That was how I had joined the group, many years earlier, when I was still a very young woman, and ever since I had followed Sarwhar with all my heart. As long as I could remember, I had yearned to have a deeper experience of Great Unity, which I had always felt to be both near and mysterious. In the village where I grew up, we had daily rituals, but my desire to know Great Unity more intimately was never completely fulfilled. So when this group arrived in our village and asked for hospitality, I felt an immediate attraction to the people and often sought their company. When they were ready to depart, I wanted to go with them. This was my chance to get closer to Great Unity, and I would be with people who felt like I did and who were led by this wonderful, charismatic man. It was hard for my parents. Their only child was leaving, perhaps forever, but they understood how much I wanted to be part of this group of seekers, and they wished me well. It was unusual for a woman to take such a step by herself. Most of the other women in the group were married or travelled with relatives. In that sense, I could be seen as ambitious, perhaps, although no one would have said that about me. On the whole, I was rather accommodating and did what was asked of me.

On the day this story begins, we had been travelling for a long time, as I said, and we were getting tired and despondent. At our prayer session that evening, Sarwhar told us he had read the signs carefully and he was sure we were on track. Some kind of significant development was not far off. Immediately, we all felt much more positive and encouraged – I told you he was a charismatic man, and we had an unshakeable trust in his leadership. We rose early the next morning. It was a beautiful day and where the terrain allowed for it, we joined hands and sang together. We often did this. They were traditional songs that made us feel at one with the soil, the sky and one another. We found a new level of strength and determination that day and made good progress. When we were setting up camp in the evening, I noticed Andisha kept herself a little apart. She was expecting, and the moment for her to give birth was not too far off, but according to our calculations there was still some time to go. I asked her if everything was all right. When she looked at me I saw that her eyes were filled with worry and tears.

'Oh Nila,' she said. 'I am afraid. I'm having contractions. They're far apart still, but I'm sure the baby is on its way. I don't think I'll be able to travel tomorrow. I'll have to have the baby here.'

Even though birth was a much more natural process for us than it is in your society, it is a big event for any woman facing it, and Andisha was very young. I was concerned that labour seemed to have started already. It was too soon, and we were several days from the nearest settlement. I put an arm round her and told her to try to get some sleep.

'Maybe it is a false alarm,' I said. 'We should wait and see how you are feeling in the morning before telling anyone.'

The next morning the contractions had become stronger, and it was clear we could not continue. Men and women usually slept in separate groups when we travelled. When the other women realised that Andisha's labour had begun, they started gathering leaves and firewood. One of the older women sat with Andisha and talked with her.

When I saw that everything was taken care of, I went to tell Janan, her husband. He had just woken up and reacted with disbelief – surely the baby was due to arrive after the next full moon? – but when he saw everyone busy round his wife, he understood. He became quite agitated, but then recovered himself and went up to Sarwhar, who was returning from his solitary early-morning prayers. It seemed to take Janan some time to make Sarwhar understand. He was gesticulating and pointing in the direction of the group of women. After a while, I saw Sarwhar nod his head and then walk off. I went back to Andisha to see if there was anything I could do for her.

She had been fourteen when we spent some time in her family's community, and she and Janan, who was part of our group, had fallen in love. There was no question in her mind that she would follow him to the ends of the Earth, and her parents had quickly arranged a wedding ceremony. She was a lovely girl who smiled often, with large eyes and long, delicate eyelashes. Janan was two years older, a serious young man, tall and muscular, completely committed to Sarwhar and finding Great Unity. Their youthful love endeared them to the group from the beginning, and everyone rejoiced with them when, after a few months, they announced they were going to have a baby.

Andisha was nervous about giving birth, and I kept her company for a while. After a few hours, the contractions became stronger, but then they eased off before stopping altogether. The women settled down. We all knew that this was how it was sometimes. It was Andisha's first baby, and conditions were not ideal. We encouraged her to assist with the meal preparation to have something to do, and we took it in turns to walk with her. The terrain was rather rocky, but flat on the whole, and we had made camp under a group of trees that provided us with shade and shelter. As the day progressed, Andisha became calmer. She understood that all of this was part of the process, and that the birth would go well if she could be patient and let nature take its course. A day passed like this, then another. On the third day, the contractions returned and they lasted all day, but they were still not very strong.

Towards the end of that day, Janan came up to me and said that Sarwhar wanted to see me. Sarwhar had come to regard me more or less as the women's representative. The other women never took the initiative to talk to him directly, and I myself didn't approach him very often, either. There had been a time when Sarwhar had desired me as his wife – at least, that was what I and most of the others had thought. Somehow, this phase had passed, and, for a while, I had been disappointed. It hadn't lasted long, and on the whole I treasured the relative freedom I enjoyed as an unmarried woman. My mother and my grandmother were midwives. They had taught me their art, and I had been present at births from when I was ten years old. Even though women were dependent on men for protection and support in our culture, my knowledge of midwifery and what you would call herbal medicine granted me a certain authority and, with that, a level of independence. My only regret was that I had no children of my own, but most of the time I was accepting of this. I saw it as my contribution to Great Unity and was glad to be of service. I had found my life-purpose in being part of this wonderful group of people who dedicated every day of their lives to Great Unity. I loved our leader, I trusted his wisdom, and was completely fulfilled following him in the way I had done for many years.

Never would I have thought that all of this would end soon.

Sarwhar was sitting under a tree a little distance away. As I approached him, I wondered what it was about him that had such appeal, even after all those years. He was well past the middle of his life – his beard and hair, which had been dark when I joined the group, had gone grey, and his face was lined – but he was still remarkably strong and hadn't lost any of the fire that had been burning inside of him for as long as I had known him. His grey eyes peered at me from under a heavy brow. They always gave away his mood. He was disgruntled. He got straight to the point, asking when the baby would be there.

'I really don't know.' I spoke deliberately and quietly, hoping to pacify him. 'It's not unusual that it happens like this. All we can do is keep up her spirits, make sure she drinks enough and walk with her.'

'Mm, if she needs walking we might as well continue, mightn't we? I mean, we could stop a bit more often to give her some rest …'

I slowly shook my head. 'I'm sorry, I understand how frustrating this must be for you, but we can't break up camp. It's true that it may take a few more days, because it seems a bit on the early side according to our calculations. But, then, calculations are not always accurate. It could be tomorrow or the next day.'

'Is there nothing you can do to speed it up?'

'I'm afraid not. The contractions could intensify at any time. Then again, they might not for a couple of days. It's impossible to say, but she can't travel, not even with extra breaks. Once labour really starts it might be fast, and then we need to be somewhere sheltered and safe to deliver the baby. I realise it must be inconvenient for you, Sarwhar, I really do, but there is nothing we can do, except trust the timing of Great Unity.'

He sighed and looked up at the heavens, lifting his palms up, as if invoking Great Unity then and there to help with a quick delivery. I was about to add something, but he had lost interest in what I might have to say.

'Please be quiet, Nila, I know enough, don't say anything more. You understand this is extremely annoying, don't you? We haven't progressed nearly as well as I had planned. A few days ago, the signs were finally favourable. I could see the direction more clearly, and the whole group responded. We made good progress that day. And now this. I'm afraid we will lose momentum.'

I said nothing. I knew him when he was soft and smiling, his eyes radiating love and understanding. It was the side of him that had instantly won me over all those years ago and made me leave my parents and everything I held dear to follow him. What I saw now was another side of him. It came to the fore whenever he felt thwarted.

The last time I had seen him like this had been a few months earlier. Arman, one of our younger men, sprained his ankle and was barely able to walk. Sarwhar told him to get himself to the settlement we had passed the previous day, because he couldn't stop the whole group just because of one person's ankle. Arman pleaded to be allowed to stay. Quite possibly, he was afraid he wouldn't make it to the settlement by himself. He was in a lot of pain. 'You can stay, of course,' Sarwhar had said, 'but we will travel at a normal pace. It's up to you to keep up.' Arman said nothing. I wrapped some palm leaves tightly round his ankle, hoping they would give some support, and he pushed himself hard. His friends carried his pack for him and urged him on. Sarwhar could be almost ruthless at times. However, he was our leader and in charge of every decision. No matter if he was caring and gentle or impatient and irritable, we followed his instructions because we firmly believed that he was directly in touch with Great Unity. He knew what was best for the group and for each of us individually. For all we knew, the sprained ankle could have been some sort of divinely inspired trial to test Arman's determination or his level of trust or his ability to follow – something like that. Who were we to know why things happened to us the way they did? We had gradually learnt not to have too many questions and to simply trust Sarwhar. Most of the time we didn't mind where we went, with whom or for how long. All we did was follow.

It's true, though, that every now and again someone joined our group who wasn't able to submit to that. I'm thinking of Ramesh. He was with us for the better part of a year. We all liked him – there was a lightness about him, and it felt good to have him around. He was serious, deep perhaps, but he was also fun to be with, his vitality as attractive as his dark wavy hair and sparkly eyes. We had spent a few days in the village where he lived with his wife and grown-up daughters. On the morning of our departure, he suddenly said he would come with us. We were surprised, but Sarwhar had smiled broadly and nodded knowingly. He had been staying with Ramesh and his family. They had one of the bigger dwellings in the village, and had been delighted to have him. I imagined how, at mealtimes, Sarwhar would have talked about our life in search of Great Unity, and I could see how this would fascinate someone like Ramesh. I looked at his wife, wondering if she would come too. But she quickly turned round and disappeared into their hut.

For a while, Ramesh was happy to be with us. He was always among the first of the men to get the fires going when we set up camp in the evening, or to encourage the others when something was bothering them. They stopped their squabbles when they saw him coming their way. Not that he ever tried to help them resolve their disagreements – he never talked a lot, in fact – but his smiling eyes made them remember the purpose of this never-ending walk. He would point at a mountain range in the distance or the reflection of the evening sun on the purple rocks, and everyone became calm, feeling the blessing of Great Unity. They admired the scenery, and remembered their gratitude for being there with Sarwhar. We all loved Ramesh.

After a few months, though, he became withdrawn. Sometimes I saw him staring into the distance and walking mechanically, unaware of the beauty of the sunset. I tried to talk to him but he insisted he was fine and was praying to Great Unity. One afternoon, I caught up with him at a moment when he was feeling particularly low, and he finally talked. 'A big change is happening inside of me, Nila,' he said. 'I remind myself this is what I wanted. Being here with Sarwhar and all of you gives me the chance I have, deep down, longed for all my life. Still, it also gives me a lot to think about, do you understand?' I made eye contact and slowly nodded.

'You know, Nila, I have always observed the laws of Great Unity. I tried to be fair and kind to people, and was respectful of the land we lived on. Now that I have been with Sarwhar for a while, I realise that I stayed at the surface of life, and was naïve in thinking that simply loving my wife and daughters and caring about others in our village would be enough. When Sarwhar stayed with us at our house and I heard him talk, I started to wonder if I should be doing something more important with my life. Until then, I appreciated everything and everyone, and thought I was happy. My family was healthy and the land was generous. But is that true happiness? Sarwhar made me see that my life had been terribly superficial. Following him, together with all of you, gives me the best chance I could ever have to change in the way I need to. But, you know, in spite of all that, I miss my wife terribly – she has always shown me so much love and wholeheartedly supported me – and my daughters, and all those times when I celebrated life with the people in my village ...'

His voice faltered, and he was overcome with emotion. I waited. The two of us had fallen to the back of the group, and there were still hours to go until we would stop for the night. We had as much time as we needed. What he said resonated with me, and I suddenly felt how much I too missed my family and what I had shared with them. For a moment, I had a profound sense of loss. I didn't allow myself to dwell on it, because I wanted to help Ramesh, and it passed quickly. Later, with hindsight, I realised that I wasn't yet ready to follow this feeling to where it would inevitably lead, so I put it away, just out of reach of my consciousness.

Ramesh continued. 'Now, I walk and pray to Great Unity, I listen to the wisdom of Sarwhar – he is such an amazing man, and I am so grateful to have met him – I sleep, pray, give thanks, walk again. Slowly, I don't know or feel anything much anymore. The other day, the thought crossed my mind that I'm becoming like the rest of you. Often you are so tired and preoccupied with what it is you are hoping to find that you don't even notice your surroundings. It is as if you have forgotten about the miracle of being alive, and it makes me wonder … for that, too, must be part of Great Unity, don't you think? If I'm totally honest, there are moments when I'm not so sure I took the right decision after all.'

Sarwhar too had noticed the change in Ramesh, and was concerned. In the evenings our leader usually kept to himself, except for an hour or so before the evening meal, when he would lead us in prayer and relay the wisdom of Great Unity. It occasionally happened that he asked one of us to join him, particularly when we were going through a difficult period or had conflicting feelings about ourselves or one of the others. He invited Ramesh to sit with him after dinner, and the group understood. Everyone had noticed that he wasn't his normal self. Several months passed like this. Sarwhar spent most evenings with Ramesh and also walked with him for a few hours each day. We could tell that they both tried, but Ramesh's eyes never smiled again, and finally, Sarwhar didn't know what to do anymore and became impatient.

There had been others who struggled, but usually these crises passed and they felt more resolve than ever. Sarwhar could not always help, though, and on rare occasions he had asked people to leave. This would cause a lot of distress, but they would come to realise that it was ultimately in their best interest. For a while, they would fight against what they saw as their resistance – somehow, they always thought it was their fault and were convinced that they were deficient in some way. Sarwhar would talk to them and remind them of the commitment they had made to themselves to seek Great Unity, and to him as the one who could guide them there. They would double their efforts to stay with the group – to follow Sarwhar and behave in the ways that were expected. But sometimes it just wasn't to be.

It was upsetting when this happened. It meant, of course, that they weren't as far advanced on the road to Great Unity as the rest of us and still had too much attachment to their former way of life, or, at least, that's what we used to think. They would leave the group as soon as was practically possible. It was often heart-breaking to say goodbye after all those years together. We naturally had become very close and we loved them as our brothers and sisters. It was much harder for the ones who left, though, because they had to rebuild their lives completely. They had lost their dream, their purpose, their homes, their closest friends and often their families. Sometimes, they found their way back to where they had come from, but often it was too far to go all that distance alone. Others felt they had been away for too long to simply go back and pick up the life they had left behind. This was what happened to Ramesh in the end. Sarwhar told him to leave, and Ramesh knew there was no other option. It took me months to stop grieving for him. It had been so good to have him with us, and he had made me think more deeply about beauty and love – what beauty and love meant to me and what place they had in our life of searching for Great Unity.

I had been sitting with Sarwhar for a long time. After he had expressed his frustration about the delay caused by Andisha's labour, our conversation had come to a halt. I wondered if there was something else he wanted to say to me, but he was staring ahead and barely seemed to notice I was still there. I decided to wait. However, after a while the silence became oppressive. It wasn't the peaceful silence that I felt with him at other times, when there was a quality of stillness that took me closer to my heart and to Great Unity. This was a different, noisy kind of silence, in which his words and my thoughts of Andisha and Ramesh and Arman were echoing. I started to feel restless and slightly nauseous. Normally, Sarwhar would be the one to end a conversation, but I felt an urgent need to be by myself. He was sitting motionless, his eyes closed. Carefully, I started to get up. I took care to move slowly, not wanting to disturb him.

'Nila!' He startled me. I turned round.

'Sarwhar, yes, is there anything else?'

'Nila, I'll wait until tomorrow morning. I don't care if the birth has happened then or not, we will carry on. I won't tolerate any more delays. Do you understand? I told you that the signs are favourable. There is no way we can let this opportunity slip by. I feel we have an incredible chance to come significantly closer to Great Unity, and we should leave at dawn.'

I looked at him in utter astonishment. At first, I thought I must have imagined his words, but I could see the exasperation on his face. He was cross with me for not seeing what to him was totally obvious and for having the temerity to think I could make him alter his plans. I had seen that expression once or twice before, a look of contempt, and I knew I had not imagined anything. He was determined, and nothing or no one was going to stop him. His patience had been stretched to the limit, and there was no room for negotiation. Something inside of me shattered, and I was overcome by dizziness. I waited, breathing slowly, until it passed. I inclined my head and walked away from him.

The sandy rock felt both soft and firm underneath my bare feet, as I walked away very slowly. I was acutely aware of life flowing through me, and all of the pores in my body opening to this miraculous energy. My breath deepened and my shoulders relaxed. I looked around me. I saw the soft light of the late afternoon reflected on the mountains in the distance, and the greyish-green hues of the leaves of the trees in whose shelter we had made our camp. Everything looked vibrant and clear. There were no thoughts, no words. Something had shattered and was no longer there. I had no idea what it was, but it wasn't a loss. Rather, it had given me space – space to feel myself, finally – and I knew I had been set free. Any sense of time or urgency had fallen away. I recognised Great Unity in all of it. I didn't quite know how or why, but I suddenly saw how it couldn't be different. I was in awe. I had found Great Unity, and it was thanks to Sarwhar, be it in a way neither of us could have ever guessed.

Would the baby be born in time? In whose time? I had attended enough births to know that it was always the baby's time. The soul that came fresh from Spirit was much more in touch with the momentous event of its own birth than anyone else ever could be. It would choose exactly the right moment. If the mother was able to trust the process, she would be in tune with the soul who had chosen to be her child, and the two of them would be able to do it together with very little help. All we needed to do was to give them all the time they needed.

Almost all women understood this naturally. For most men, it wasn't like that, but usually they were respectful of women's intuition in these matters – and often a bit scared as well – and didn't interfere. That Sarwhar didn't have that respect had shocked me to the core. Sarwhar, of all people, whom I had admired and followed with all my heart for so long. Whom I had loved. However, the shattering had changed everything. I felt completely at one with Great Unity, and I was sure that, in its boundless compassion, Great Unity would also be with Sarwhar.

That evening, when we were sitting round the fires, Sarwhar announced that we would depart early the next morning. Most people looked pleased. This hadn't been an interesting or comfortable place to stay for several days. A few looked around for Andisha. Everyone knew we were waiting for her to give birth, and they assumed the baby must have been born in the course of that day. She was sitting not far from me, looking at me with terror in her big brown eyes. 'Surely, there is a mistake?' those eyes seemed to say. 'Surely our leader knows my baby is on its way and that we have to wait for it? Wait for me?'

'It will be all right,' I mouthed. The contractions had stopped again a few hours ago, and she looked panic-stricken. One of the women who sat next to her started rubbing her back. As more people saw Andisha sitting there with us, still very much pregnant, they looked puzzled. No one dared saying anything.

Sarwhar was the only one who was unperturbed, a faint smile playing on his lips. 'I am waiting,' he said, after what felt like a very long time. 'I am waiting for you to finally stop the chatter and the noise in your heads. Please let's not be distracted. This is a crucial point in time. As I told you before, the signs have never been better. Look up at the stars! They are perfectly aligned. Early tomorrow morning, we will start crossing the stretch of desert between here and the mountains. It will take us two days. Once we are there, the secrets of the universe will be revealed to us, I'm certain of it. I have a feeling that Great Unity will address us directly. We are about to experience something absolutely unique. The last time any of this eternal knowledge was revealed to human beings was several hundred years ago. No one has been judged worthy to receive it since. We are the chosen ones.'

Everyone was dumbfounded. They could hardly take it in. After so many years of relentless walking, of quietly doubting at times and wondering if it wouldn't be better to settle somewhere and have a more ordinary life, they were about to see the fruit of their efforts, the reward for their unwavering commitment. Some of them were sobbing with emotion, nearly all had tears in their eyes.

'Thank you, Sarwhar,' someone managed to say. 'Thank you for never losing sight of the goal. Thank you for guiding us!'

Other voices joined his. 'Thank you, Sarwhar, thank you!'

Our leader looked around the circle, briefly nodding in acknowledgement.

'What about my wife? What about my child?'

Most of the others had forgotten Andisha's predicament and seemed reluctant to let this magnificent moment be spoiled. All eyes were on Sarwhar; how was he going to solve this?

Sarwhar addressed Janan directly. 'We can wait no longer,' was all he said. 'I have just explained that. I trust you heard me. Whoever wants to meet Great Unity should be ready to join me at dawn. If you want to continue the journey with me, this is your chance. I will not wait.'

He got up and started to walk away.

I was surprisingly calm, certain that Great Unity was not two days' walk away. However, I knew that we needed help with the birth, and people to accompany us afterwards. I got up. 'Sarwhar! All of you! Please listen!'

Everyone looked at me in surprise. Sarwhar stopped in his tracks and turned round, slightly bemused.

'We cannot leave without Andisha, and Andisha cannot leave,' I began. 'For goodness' sake, come to your senses! We cannot in good conscience simply walk away from her. I cannot believe that any of you would even consider for a moment that this could be an option. Andisha and Janan are part of us. Do you remember how glad you all were when they first told us about the child that would come into their lives? Into our lives? How we all felt blessed? Janan and Andisha want to find Great Unity as much as any of us. Please, let's wait for them.'

Everyone was astonished to hear me speak like this. As I told you in the beginning, I was mostly quiet. All I wanted was to follow Sarwhar, just like the others. That's how it had been for years. Until that afternoon. No one knew, of course, about my realisation about Great Unity, and this obviously wasn't the time to tell anyone. I looked at Andisha, how beautiful she was, how afraid and vulnerable with her baby inside of her. I thought of Ramesh, who had said that the miracle of life surely must be part of Great Unity too. Everything fell into place. Sarwhar, despite his wisdom, didn't realise that Great Unity was not across the desert at the foot of the mountains, but in the new life about to be born and in each of the loyal followers he had guided for such a great distance. I felt carried along by the force of Great Unity and continued.

'Please, stay to greet Andisha's baby. It comes straight from Great Unity to be here with us. Help us celebrate its arrival and make it feel welcome.' The people looked from me to Sarwhar, from Sarwhar to me. Most sensed that something wasn't right. On the other hand, Sarwhar was always right, and he was certainly right now, given what he had just told them. He simply had to be. And there was something else: no one ever argued with Sarwhar, and I was one of the last people anyone would have expected to do so.

There was a long silence. Then Sarwhar finally spoke. 'It's up to you if you want to come with us or not, Nila.' Anger was clouding his face at being challenged like this in front of everyone – by me, a woman. A woman he had once desired as his wife. 'I don't know what has got into you that you think you know better than I. There are much more important things in life than the simple, everyday events you seem to be concerned about. It saddens me that after all these years you still haven't learnt that. Everyone moves at their own pace, however, and I bless you all the same. Those of you who want to join me in going to the mountains to receive the secrets of the universe should be ready to leave at first light. I wish you all a good night.'

He walked away. It was the last I saw of him in that life.

When Sarwhar had disappeared, I took my place in the circle again with the others. For a while, no one spoke and no one moved. No one dared look at me. Gradually, one after the other, people left to prepare for the night. In the end, only Andisha and Janan, Janan's brother and his wife, and Gulrang, one of the older women remained. She was a widow and my best friend. They all said they would stay. We moved closer to Andisha, held hands and sang and prayed to Great Unity. Then we went to sleep.

I woke to the noise of people placing water bags and other supplies near our small group. Janan had asked them for those the night before, and fortunately they had remembered. I thanked them, and one of them mumbled something in reply before scurrying off. How strange! We had shared everything with these people for years and years and now they were behaving as if we had a contagious disease.

Not long after, I saw them gathering in the distance. Some of them cast us a furtive glance. I imagined that, deep inside, they were torn between their conscience and their profound commitment to following Sarwhar. I was sure, though, that once they were on their way, those conflicting feelings would subside. I knew all too well how persuasive and irresistible Sarwhar's confidence could be. They called out to a couple of dawdling women to hurry up, and then they helped each other to hoist their packs onto their backs and began walking east, without looking back. The others had woken up and together we watched the people most dear to us walk out of our lives without a word of farewell.

'Nila…?' It was Andisha. The contractions had come back. 'They are so strong, I'm not sure I can take it.'

'You can, Andisha. It's good news, you know. It means the baby is coming. It won't be long now.'

The men started another fire and the women supported Andisha. Her labour progressed well now, and a few hours later the baby came out smoothly. It was a perfect birth. The little boy was serene when I caught him and passed him to his mother, the umbilical cord still intact. He started drinking immediately, and she looked at him in awe, stroking him tenderly, tears streaming down her cheeks, all the worries of the past days and the pain of labour instantly forgotten.

'We should call him Baddar,' she smiled through her tears, 'because he came both early and exactly at the right time.' She looked at me meaningfully, and I understood that she too had discovered the truth about Great Unity. We smiled broadly at each other as we welcomed Baddar and gave thanks to Great Unity.

THE BIRTH OF BADDAR

The next day, Andisha put Baddar in a sling and we set off. At first, we just backtracked, then after a couple of days we veered west, where we knew there was a small settlement. With Andisha and the baby, we could only go slowly, but we didn't mind. Each of us in our own way needed time to fully come to terms with what had happened. Our lives had changed from one day to the next. Every step took us further from Sarwhar and closer to life without him. Baddar had joined us on Earth just as Sarwhar left us, and this felt somehow significant. He was a beautiful, peaceful baby, his eyes wide open most of the time, reflecting the spirit of Great Unity.

Those days of travelling, just the six of us and the baby, are forever etched in my memory. I had a feeling of total peace. In the afternoon of the fourth day we arrived at the settlement. It was small, but inviting, and the people were friendly. They looked at Baddar with wonder and delight – such a small baby, fresh from Great Unity! They prepared a delicious meal as a welcome and assured us we could stay for as long as we needed. We gratefully accepted their hospitality and stayed with them for ten days. After that, our lives took us in different directions.

It was completely silent in the room. No one moved or coughed or looked around. After a while, I wondered if Nila was still there, and I looked at Ian. He too had been motionless, but I saw he was smiling and looking at us from under half-raised eyelids.

'I'm still here,' his voice said. I knew it was Nila speaking, and I was glad. 'Is there anything you would like to ask?'

Richard put up his hand. 'Nila – is it all right if I call you Nila? Could you please talk a bit more about Ramesh? Why did he join your group so suddenly, and what happened to him afterwards?'

Richard had spent years in Buddhist monasteries in Thailand. He had joined our group only recently, and I didn't know him as well as I knew most of the others. He owned some land in the hilly countryside about an hour out of town, where he ran classes in meditation and Qi gong. I wondered if he too had left a woman to pursue his spiritual quest. He had been unusually quick to raise his hand.

'I understand why you'd like to call me Nila, and it doesn't matter what you call me, as long as it's clear that I speak as part of Consciousness. In the story, my consciousness expressed itself as the person called Nila. Now that I am in Spirit, I have joined a much wider pool of Consciousness, although not nearly the largest. There is still much for me to discover. When I say "my" consciousness, it's not correct, actually. There is only Consciousness, no one has exclusive rights, but it's easier for you when I explain it like this. I'm sorry, I don't mean to be particular, and you are really very welcome to call me Nila. It's just that your question of what name to call me by gives me an opportunity to remind you not to identify too much with your personality or your physical body. By all means, love the persona you have chosen to express through, and have a good time with him or her, but don't forget that there is another truth to who you are. Your true nature has no name.

'But you asked about Ramesh … I'm sorry, I digressed. I said at the beginning that the spotlight would be on Sarwhar and Nila, but, in fact, Ramesh was also a key player. As was Baddar by the way, who chose to be born early as far as his due date was concerned, but in actual fact at precisely the right time to create a profoundly significant experience for Nila and Andisha. So, Ramesh … Ramesh was a very gentle soul. Before entering into life, he had made an agreement with Sarwhar. The plan was to overcome the last vestiges of a tendency for him to doubt what he knew deep inside to be true. When he first met Sarwhar, he was led to believe that Great Unity was somewhere far away, and finding it became more urgent than anything else. During the long days of walking, he realised how much he loved his family and the life he had led in his community. In the end, he recognised that he had made a mistake, and was overwhelmed with grief for what he had lost. In the long, painful process that followed, he was to remember that Great Unity is everywhere, and that it never asks you to leave the people you love.

'Many souls in this group of followers, myself included, had similar life-lessons, to do with the need to discover our own truth – and by that I mean that which deeply, genuinely resonates with each of us – and to not give up on it, no matter what others might tell us. Ramesh was much closer to this than the rest of us, and this was why it was such a struggle for him. He suffered from being so keenly aware of the dichotomy between the reality of this relentless quest and his increasing sense that it didn't feel right. Because of his karmic connection with Sarwhar he trusted him completely, and this was why he fought his feelings for so long. It never occurred to him that he might know something that Sarwhar did not. And, of course, exactly herein lay his test.

'When he finally left the group, he was convinced that he was an utter failure who had lost his only chance to achieve what he desired most. What else could there possibly be, after forgoing such an opportunity? What was wrong with him that he could not do what all the others in the group did so easily? Why was it so hard for him to stop having all those other feelings? He stayed in the first settlement he reached. He was depressed by then and had no idea what else to do. In the beginning, he sat under a tree for most of the day, staring ahead of him. The people in that community were curious about the group of seekers he had belonged to, and asked him about it. Eventually, he began to talk, and gradually he started to understand what had happened. Some of his new friends greatly admired him for making finding Great Unity the most important thing in his life, and a few of them wondered if they shouldn't pack up and do the same. However, most of them gently affirmed Ramesh's feelings, simply by being who they were. As he witnessed their daily life, with its relationships, activities and celebrations, his love of life rekindled. The day finally came when he announced that he would be leaving to find his family. He thanked the people in the community for giving him the help he so badly needed when he first arrived, and for showing him that there was no conflict between leading a joyful life and honouring Great Unity. "I would gladly have stayed with you here," he said, "but I have to go back to my wife and daughters …"'

Sonia got in quickly at that point. 'And? Did he? Get back to his wife and daughters?'

'Yes, he did in the end. It was a very long way, however, and by the time he returned to his village several years had passed, and not everything was as he had left it. His wife had taken his sudden departure very badly and never totally recovered. Other people who were dear to him had changed. Naturally, life doesn't stand still. His daughters needed quite some time to overcome their resentment of him for leaving them and their mother, but in the end they warmed towards him. The most wonderful thing was being with his grandchildren. They were too young to know what had happened and quickly grew fond of this grandfather who had suddenly appeared and was fun to be with. He played with them endlessly, or they went on long walks, and when they were tired they would sit on his lap or at his feet while he told them about Great Unity – that it was everywhere, in every rock and bit of bark, and particularly in their hearts and the hearts of their parents and everyone in their village. When they were older, he often spoke of the time when he had left their mothers and their grandmother whom he loved so much, and it would always cause him deep emotion. But he knew with quiet certainty that it had been right for him to join Sarwhar and right for him to abandon him when he did. He was at peace and lived a fulfilled life in his community.'

Nila laughed softly when she spoke those last words. 'I'm sure you like this bitter-sweet happy ending. And before you ask … no,

I'm sorry, I won't tell you more. I think you've got enough to think about.'

I found myself imagining Ramesh with his grandchildren. I also wondered about his wife and how she might have been affected by his years of absence, but it seemed Nila thought other things were more important.

'How can you ever know if a decision is right? You say Ramesh learnt what he had planned to learn, and I can see that because of the way you told the story. But it looks to me as if, on a personal level, he made all the wrong decisions.' It was Ralph, who seemed to be struggling.

'Wrong decisions?'

'Well, yes. I mean, he leaves his village and then goes back years later to find that his marriage is more or less over. Also, he wasn't with the others when they had the revelation from Great Unity. Wasn't that a mistake? Going all that way, making all those sacrifices, and then missing out on that great moment? I can't help thinking it was an awfully long detour.'

'My dear friend, I assure you it wasn't quite like that. I am sorry if this disappoints you, perhaps, but, for a start, there was no revelation from Great Unity. At least, not then and not in the way they thought. Also, please don't be too worried about what you might call detours. It's hard to know if you detour or not, if you are not sure where you are going. All you can do is continue on the path on which you find yourself. The experiences you gather will eventually provide you with certain insights. Those insights will help you further, and gradually the path will become easier. It is, however, the nature of the human journey in the dimension of physicality to have all kinds of experiences and to learn by trial and error. If Ramesh, instead of going with Sarwhar, had stayed in his community, he would have had similar experiences in another way, or maybe in another life, because, as a soul, it was his wish to strengthen his trust in his own knowing. Actually, what you call Ramesh's detour is an example of a life-learning that went completely according to plan. He came to understand that the life he had led in his community with his family had been perfect. This whole episode brought him the confirmation which, on a soul level, he had sought.

'Ramesh and Sarwhar are very close souls. You have met them already, in fact, in the Valley of Plenty, when they were both further along in their soul development. They met only briefly then, but long enough to remind each other of the core of their respective life-issues. As the Wanderer, the soul we met today as Sarwhar challenged his host, who was another soul-expression of Ramesh, by asking repeatedly if there was really nothing else he desired in life. This time, the latter was without a single doubt that living in the valley with the people he loved was deeply meaningful, and that there was nothing else he needed. In turn, he was to show his guest that everything he so deeply yearned for was right there and there was no need for him to keep on searching – he even invited him to stay. Remember the repetitive nature of their conversations? They were very thorough!

'We know from the valley story that the learning was resolved for the soul who expressed as the host – Ramesh in today's story – and that the Wanderer was to explore further his idea that there might be something more desirable somewhere else. We all arrive at our destination eventually. There is no competition, only mutual support. The host in the valley, who in his life as Ramesh learnt a hard lesson, lived to a ripe old age without ever doubting that living in love and gratitude was all that mattered. Oh, and there's one more thing. I myself, or, rather, the soul who has been speaking to you as Nila tonight and to whom Ramesh poured out his heart in the desert, was his wife in that life in the valley. I can confirm from personal experience that it was a totally fulfilling, very happy life.'

I was terribly excited to hear about Nila and Ramesh – or whatever they might have been called at various times. I considered the reciprocal life-lessons we had just heard about: Nila and Sarwhar first of all, but also Sarwhar and Ramesh. Ramesh and Nila seemed to have had a different kind of soul relationship. They were like-minded souls who supported each other during their quest in the desert and then found each other again to celebrate happiness, love and abundance in the valley. I felt Elspeth's eyes on me and we smiled at each other. It was good to know that, apart from the many painful lessons we seemed to inflict upon one another, there was that other side: one of quiet, fulfilled love and deep mutual understanding. I would have been happy to go home on this note, but Herman had another question for Nila.

'I'm not sure that I understand what exactly it was that shattered inside of you. Could you please talk about that a bit more?'

'Yes, certainly. Life's lessons are often strangely convoluted. In the story you just heard, I was pulled so far out of my heart that something snapped, just like a piece of elastic snapping when you stretch it too much. I needed to be shunted back to what was true for me, and it was through Sarwhar that I had this break-through. He helped me overcome a belief I had carried with me for much of my soul history. When he and I were talking about Andisha, he stated so powerfully and unequivocally what he held to be true at that moment, which was so different from what I believed, that it provoked my own knowing to shout out, as it were. What shattered was my belief that my truth was somehow inferior to someone else's. Suddenly, I found myself in the middle of my heart. I could feel life flowing through me and my confidence returning. I had followed Sarwhar for years, expecting that he would lead me to Great Unity, to the essence of who I am, as you may think of it. It was miraculous that he did just that, and that it happened exactly when it became clear to me I could no longer follow him. I needed this kind of shock treatment to reconnect with myself, and it was Sarwhar who provided that treatment. For too long, I had ignored the knowing of my heart by referring to others as authorities.

'Interestingly enough, most people intuitively know what you mean when you speak of the heart. So many everyday expressions in your language bear witness to that: heart-warming, disheartening, light-hearted, openhearted, heartstrings, heartfelt … It shows how, collectively, you never completely lost the heart connection. Through a long process of conditioning, most people do not trust their heart, which they think of as "only a feeling". When I met Sarwhar, who was so confident about finding Great Unity, and fell under the spell of his charisma – and also, possibly, because he was interested in me as a woman – I assumed that his knowing would be much more reliable than my own. As I followed him more, I listened to my own heart less, so much so that I thought I needed him to show me what life was about. And he did do that in the end, even if it was in a very different way than either of us could have predicted. In subsequent lives, I learnt to be much more in touch with my intuitive knowing. It would be tested heavily at times, but since that experience I never completely forgot that guidance can always be found in my own heart.'

'Wow, Nila, that's very powerful,' said Herman. 'I've never realised that we support others when we behave in ways that cause conflict. It's encouraging. Makes me think that maybe I should stop trying to be nice all the time … hmm … I'll need to give that some thought. Thank you so much for sharing this with us! I wonder, would you mind terribly if I ask another question, please?'

Ian gestured for someone to refill the carafe on the table beside him. It had been a long evening, but he didn't want to end it yet. He was as fascinated as the rest of us by the convoluted methods of the universe and the power of the heart. Someone fetched water and then Herman asked his next question.

'You said in the beginning it was about a reciprocal lesson. Could you tell us what it was that Sarwhar learnt from you?'

Ian nodded and his body started to gently rock. He seemed to be waiting for Nila, who didn't speak for quite a while. For a moment, I thought she might have gone, but then she spoke again.

'Yes, yes, sure ... Let me see ... I wonder if perhaps ... yes, good ... he's just let me know ... and our medium is willing too, I feel ... yes ... Sarwhar will tell you about this himself. I will make room for him. It was lovely meeting you all. I hope our story will help you find the way to your hearts more often. Don't be afraid to act upon what you find there.'

'Thank you, Nila.' We said it all together.

'My very great pleasure,' she answered, and that was the last we heard from her.

Ian moved in his chair and drank some water. He looked at us briefly and closed his eyes again. It hardly took any time at all before the soul who had walked the Earth as Sarwhar started to speak.

'Oh my goodness! It's true what Nila said at the start of your evening – that I could have told you the story from my point of view and it would have been very different. I don't think I'll need to do that. I'm sure you can imagine what it would have been like.' He laughed. Apparently, he thought it was amusing. I wondered if that is what it is like to look back on our lives on Earth, once our soul doesn't return here anymore. It felt a bit like a mature adult looking back on the antics of childhood and not taking any of it too seriously.

'For quite a long time in my soul history,' he continued, 'I had the rather fixed-but-false idea that there must be something much better and worthier in life, and I always assumed that it was to be uncovered in some far-away, hard-to-find place. You heard about this when I was stumbling around in those mountains in another life. It's central to the lives of all human beings, this looking outside of yourself for happiness or love or fulfilment. It's the most immediate consequence of our separation from Source. Separation itself is only an idea – we've told you about that – but it's nevertheless a compelling way of looking at reality when you live in physicality. For me, this sense of missing something vital was much more urgent than it is for most people. That's why you see in my soul history so many extensive, perilous journeys.' He smiled. 'Not that it was all useless, mind you. Every experience gave me a chance to see life from another angle. I didn't always recognise it, but all those angles added up and gradually contributed to the realisation that I am a divine creature and not lacking in anything. When that finally happened, I felt indescribable joy. It was a mind-blowing experience – I mean that almost literally. But I am getting ahead of myself here. I just wanted to reassure you that, ultimately, every story has a happy ending. Eternity is taking care of that, ha-ha. For now, let's return to the life when I was Sarwhar.

'Coming back to your question about this reciprocal learning … when Nila spoke to me and the rest of the group that evening around the fires in the desert, she appealed to our hearts. I was so single-mindedly preoccupied with the idea of finding Great Unity that I had forgotten what it actually meant. I had lost sight of its depth and vastness and its all-encompassing love. Over time, Great Unity had become nothing but a goal to be achieved, and I forgot all about compassion. That was unfortunate, it really was. I couldn't see that the shortest route to Great Unity would have been through welcoming Baddar, who came fresh from Spirit, and through supporting his mother, who was frightened and vulnerable. I should have remembered that Great Unity is to be found in the other who stands before me, not over the next mountain range. It was a huge blind spot, all things considered – wanting to find the divine and, in my zeal, looking away from the needs of the people around me.' He slowly shook his head and was quiet for a while.

'The mutual agreement between Nila and me was that I would try to force her to do something so far removed from what she knew in her heart to be true that it could only propel her back into the depths of her own inner knowing. That's the part she has told you. Her role was to remind me, in any way she could, of the reality of love as opposed to a mere concept of it. We could have married, had children, but I lacked the courage to love and be loved. I didn't trust my heart very much then, and too often I took refuge in the mind. Nila was to bring me back to the realisation that Great Unity is about love and compassion in the here and now, not in omens or revelations that point to a place and time in the future. However, it didn't quite work out the way we planned. There are always variables, and the outcomes of our escapades into physicality are largely left open. It was a major block in my soul history, and it took me quite a few lives until it was finally resolved. Every time I experienced an action that came from love or a more felt, nuanced state of being, a little piece was chipped away from the block. That's how it happens for most of us when we work towards letting go of deep-seated life-issues.

'When you listen to the story-as-a-story, you might feel judgmental of Sarwhar. I stopped identifying with him long ago, so don't worry, I understand your feelings. This story shows you to what extent our actions on Earth are intertwined with those of others. More often than not, souls significantly contribute to each other by taking roles that don't make them exactly popular by earthly standards. So, yes, you are right,' he added, addressing Herman, 'there is no need to always be nice.' He laughed again.

'We tell you these stories about real people – their joys, their desires, their despair – because we want you to move further into your hearts. Your mind, your capacity to think and analyse and form concepts, is a useful tool. It's just that its importance has become overrated, and it's the heart that is the gateway to understanding your true nature – what we used to call Great Unity. In simple terms: feeling is crucially important! There is a fast-developing movement in your twenty-first century that seeks to underpin this scientifically. Their research should convince people who are overly reliant on their mental faculties that the voice of the heart is real. Once the balance between thinking and feeling has been restored, people can be more discerning and less susceptible to being led astray.'

We all knew what he meant. A week earlier we had gone for a drink after our session, and we had talked about the kind of research Sarwhar seemed to be referring to. Jason had told us about a documentary he had seen, which showed that the heart and the brain communicate, and that this communication is instigated by the heart, not the brain. The brain releases its chemicals according to the instructions of the heart. This means that the brain's choice of which chemicals to release is directly influenced by our feelings at that moment. Positive feelings, like gratitude or compassion, cause the brain to release substances that stimulate the immune system, and other substances that are good for us. Emotions like anxiety or anger result in stress hormones being released, which ultimately undermine physical health. Apparently, this is now measurable or at least observable. We had all thought this an exciting development. Science and spirituality supporting and complementing each other seemed in itself a way towards redressing the imbalance between heart and mind.

I had missed a bit, and Sarwhar was now talking about 'truth'. As I listened, I started to get an idea of how subjective truth really is and how easily it can be made into a concept or precept that is held up to others to believe in and follow.

'In my life as Sarwhar, when Baddar was born to Andisha, I had no idea yet of the relative nature of truth, and I very much thought in terms of black and white. Because I was such an earnest seeker and my goal was so compelling, others put their trust in me. They thought, as I did myself, that "following" meant to be compliant, but of course it isn't like that at all. Following certain beliefs or values, or another human being, isn't something you should do blindly, and no matter what someone else tells you or how well intended they are, you must always consult your own intelligence and weigh up their words in your heart. I didn't know any of that, though. In time, most of the people who chose to follow me in that life lost all confidence in their own knowing and even in the validity of their feelings and personal experiences. The wisdom of the universe can take unexpected turns, however, and in the end it was through a kind of reverse psychology that I guided Nila to her heart. I wasn't conscious of applying any psychology, needless to say, nor of any guiding, for that matter, but that's what happened. I'm so glad that I could do that for her. I did more or less the same for Ramesh and, to a lesser extent, for some of the others.

'It would be fair to say that much of the action during my life as Sarwhar was dramatic, and there were distressing lessons for many in that group. I myself had to face a devastating lesson in humility a few years after my clash with Nila about Baddar's birth. I had started out with a genuine desire to lead others to the realisation of their divine nature, and perhaps I could have done that, but in the end I fell in love with my elevated status and was blinded by it. Great mindfulness is needed to bear the admiration of others and not be seduced by the egoic need for more of it. I should have known that the universe always tests us on our true motives when we take on great responsibilities, and I clearly failed that test.

'I took the lesson to heart as much as was possible in the span of a lifetime. Many of the others too had crushing experiences. Sometimes, lives are like that. Other times, they are more easy-going. I pushed myself hard in most of my lives. Only towards the end of my reincarnation cycle did I start to see it isn't necessary to put in quite so much effort – that, in fact, you have a better chance of progressing by doing less and having a little more trust that life will support and steer you. However, I got there in the end. I will leave you with that. It will be bedtime soon in your corner of the planet. Thank you for listening. Perhaps we'll meet again.'

THE BLUE STONE

The path becomes clearer

It was our first time back after the summer break, the smell of autumn already in the air. Our sessions always broke up for several months so that Ian could spend time with his elderly mother, who lived in the far south, and go tramping with a childhood friend in a forest area where they could walk for days without seeing anyone. I had spent many wonderful, lazy days with Colin and his best friend, Tommy, at the beach. Later, when Fred took Colin on a camping trip with his cousins, I used the time to myself to try out recipes based on the ancient grains I had recently discovered. Hearing about the golden-stemmed barley in the Garden of Plenty and the tastes and textures that the Wanderer had so much appreciated had awakened in me an interest in grains. Some were supposed to have great health benefits, and after experimenting with farro and amaranth and a few other types I hadn't even heard of, I became excited about their versatility and was considering making them the theme for my next book.

It felt like a long time since we had last spoken with our spirit friends, but our first visitor in many weeks put us quickly back in the picture.

'Good evening! I know you are not in a position to recognise me, but we have met before. I told you about the soul who wandered into that fertile valley one day and struggled with the feeling that something essential was missing in his life. I was his guide, appearing as an old man with a twinkle in his eye. Not long before your summer break, you heard about another life of his, when he led a group of people who were searching for Great Unity. Today, we would like to give you one more episode about him, highlighting events that took place much later in his soul history. As witnesses, in a manner of speaking, you will have a chance to appreciate the kind of learning process that takes place throughout a reincarnation cycle.'

Witnesses ... yes, indeed, that's what we were. I was suddenly filled with images ... of that isolated community in Lozeh's movie about the nature of good and evil – it had been a long time ago, but I saw it in vivid detail – with the trance-inducing drumming, and Ardashir rummaging through his basket of magic herbs in order to 'cure' Navīd ... of the trees laden with apples and apricots in the Garden of Plenty with its clear mountain streams, the concentrated look on the faces of the children engrossed in building their creations with sand and pebbles ... the Wanderer and the Old Man, deep in conversation despite their perilous position in those forsaken mountains ... and Nila, slowly walking away after her confrontation with Sarwhar in the desert, feeling liberated and forever changed. Indeed, it felt as if I had been there. These weren't ordinary story-telling evenings – more like dreams, perhaps. I had done a lot of reading on the beach, always with one eye on the boys in the water with their boogie boards, and one of my books had been about dreams. It said that experiences in a dream state are often as real as the ones we have when we are awake, if not more so. Could the same be said of these stories?

THE BLUE STONE

'Exploration of Consciousness often involves faraway places, intriguing people, landscapes or objects, and profound experiences along the way. Not that it's necessary to go to such lengths, far from it, but this was the way of this particular soul, and it's true that it offers chances for good story-telling. Even though travelling can broaden the mind, if you forgive us that expression, the most important journey is the journey within. Eventually, our protagonist will discover this for himself. Before that happens, one more adventure awaits him...

He is on another quest, as you have come to expect from him. This time, we find him searching for a stone, for the perfect Blue Stone. During a large part of his life, he can be seen digging into the earth – hills, mountains, sandy deserts – or staring intently into creeks and puddles on stony plains. He searches methodically and efficiently. His eyesight is sharp and attuned to the colour blue, which you don't see much in this part of the world, except for the sky, which is mostly cloudless. Shades of brown, grey and yellow, along with the dusty greens of the vegetation, are the predominant colours of this desert-like landscape. The seeker is no longer young, but not yet old, either. He is of slight build, wiry and resilient. His hands are strong and his fingers are tough, but also sensitive and agile. There is a look of intensity in his eyes, which are dark and deep-set. Every now and again, when he relaxes, they suddenly soften, showing the gentle, somewhat shy man he is. He uses the best hours of the day, and when his eyes are too tired to be reliable he closes them and rests. He is determined to fulfil his task. Not many blue stones escape his scrutiny, and over time he finds some that are truly spectacular. None is ever deemed perfect by the Master, however. For it is the Master who has urged him to go on this quest for the ultimate Blue Stone. Each time the Master dismisses a stone because it is not the right one, beautiful as it may be, he encourages him to keep on searching.

After many, many years, during which he finds some astonishing stones that are nonetheless rejected by the Master, and after suffering prolonged periods of frustration and downheartedness and every imaginable kind of difficulty, the day comes when, at the edge of the desert, on the lower slope of a mountain, his trained eye detects a trace of an unusual blue caught by a ray of sunlight. The shimmering colour takes his breath away, and his head starts spinning. He steadies himself before climbing towards it, keeping his eyes focused on the spot. He squats down right in front of it and slowly and very gently teases the stone out of the mountain, carefully pushing aside other, lesser stones. It offers little resistance and slides easily into the palm of his hand.

He needs only one look to know that this stone is unlike any he has seen before. It is a wonderfully rich, sparkling blue, like turquoise but deeper, with three delicate, golden lines on one side. As it is resting in his hand, he feels its energy pulsating: the stone is talking to him. He sinks down and wipes it clean with his hand, then uses his sleeve to polish it with a bit of spit. He can't take his eyes off the dazzling blue, its shades changing as the light of the sun plays on it. He sighs. It truly is perfect. This must be the stone the Master spoke of, the stone he was to find. No wonder the Master had not accepted any of the stones he had brought him earlier. The treasure that is resting in his hand far surpasses them all. His quest has finally come to an end.

He sits on the slope for a long time, oblivious to the heat of the day, the setting of the sun, the coolness of the evening. He can't believe that, after all this time, he has found the Stone of Stones. Time and again, he looks at the stone in the palm of his hand, entranced by its mysterious presence, imagining the look on the Master's face when he sees this unspeakable beauty. That night, he cannot sleep, his heart overflowing with excitement and gratitude.

The next day, he starts off to the house of the Master, a good ten days on foot. His step is light and so is his heart, in anticipation of the moment when he will hand over the stone to the Master, his mission finally completed. One beautiful afternoon, he reaches the Master's house at the edge of a small settlement. The landscape is dry and dusty, but the Master's needs are few, and it's a beautiful spot, with the mountains visible in the distance. Two students are sitting in front of the house. A third one is sweeping up some leaves. They greet him respectfully, and one of them hurries inside and returns with a jug of cool water and some dates. He graciously accepts and smiles, but doesn't speak. He has not spoken since he found the stone. It is as if speaking would somehow diminish the enormity of his at long last finding the Blue Stone.

After a meal of vegetable soup prepared by the students, he is invited to see the Master. His heart starts beating faster. He breathes slowly, trying to calm himself before entering the room he knows so well. Remembering to duck down as he passes through the doorway, he pauses for a moment. The Master's wrinkled face lights up when he sees him, and it strikes him how much he has aged. With pain in his heart, he realises that the man who in many ways has been like a father to him might not be on Earth for very much longer. The Master is sitting cross-legged on a cushion, exuding serenity. His silver-white hair touches his shoulders – a few strands still cover his crown, making him look vulnerable and precious like a new-born baby. The Master gestures for him to sit down on a cushion close to his, and he inclines his head in thanks before lowering himself. It has been nearly two years since he last saw the Master, two years since he last found a stone he hoped would be worthy of his approval. He has missed him, and he feels how much good it does him to be in his presence. Being with the Master quietens his mind and anchors him in himself. For a long while they sit without speaking, sipping the acacia-leaf tea one of the students has brought them. Then the Master looks up at him, and there is such a gentle glow in his eyes, and his warm smile feels so welcoming, that he wishes this moment would last forever. The Master starts to speak, his voice soft, but steady.

'My dear friend,' he says, 'I am so very glad to see you again. It has been a long time. How have you been?' He sizes him up as he speaks, nods his head thoughtfully and looks his visitor in the eye. 'Would you like to tell me about your travels? About what you have learnt, what you have found?'

The man who found the Blue Stone lowers his gaze. He hesitates, suddenly overwhelmed. From a fold in his robes, he very slowly takes the Blue Stone and shows it to the Master. The Master takes it from him with great care and examines it meticulously. He feels its weight in one hand, then in the other, turns it over this way and that, stroking it lovingly. Holding it lightly between his thumb and index finger, he brings it towards his face to look at it closely, then lifts it up to the light. Lastly, he presses it gently against his chest, his eyes closed.

Finally, he speaks. 'What a beautiful stone you found, my friend, a truly exquisite stone, its shape outstandingly balanced, its colour a glorious blue. What a joy to look at, what a treasure. What a magnificent find! Thank you, thank you so much!' He strokes the stone again. Then he carefully puts it next to their tea bowls on a piece of willow-wood with peeling bark that serves as a table. It is the only object in the room, apart from an earthy-red rug that covers some of the sandstone floor and the cushions they are sitting on – and the Master's bed in the far corner. They sit for a long time, in perfect, companionable silence, contemplating the gorgeous shades of blue.

At last, the Master speaks again. 'My friend, you found a remarkable stone. It is unique. I have never seen one like it. I am very, very impressed with it. Even so … I can't help it, I must tell you … this is not what I asked you to find. No … not at all … not at all …' He gently shakes his head as he utters these words.

The other feels as if the ground is disappearing from under him. Surely there is a mistake. He has not heard properly, or perhaps the Master is now so old that he has forgotten what he asked him to do all those years ago. He knows in his heart that there is no more beautiful stone to be found anywhere in the world, that he has found the most magnificent stone the Earth could ever yield. This was his task, and he has fulfilled it. The Master must have lost his mind.

Then he sees in the eyes of the Master a faint glimmer. Is he mocking him? He looks again and sees gentleness and endless compassion.

'I am so very sorry,' the Master says slowly, 'I know you think you have found the most magnificent stone the Earth could ever yield. And in a way, it is true. But in another way, it is not. You must continue your search.'

The man gets to his feet with great difficulty. He tries to thank the Master, but his voice has deserted him, and all he can do is give him a forlorn look before leaving the room. He spends a sleepless night with the students in the hut next to the Master's house. The next day, he leaves at dawn, never to return.

When he leaves the house of the Master, he is without hope. The purpose of a lifetime appears never to have existed. There is no blue stone that is The Blue Stone. There certainly are blue stones that are superb in a variety of ways, and he has found quite a few of those. He even found the Most Magnificent Stone the Earth Could Ever Yield, the ultimate Blue Stone – he is sure of that – but it wasn't what the Master meant. What, then, had he meant? Why would the Master ask him to spend his life looking for the most exquisite stone, only to tell him it wasn't what he really meant when he finally found it? He had loved the Master, and he still loves him. He can't imagine that the Master would play tricks on him. That he would send him on a lifelong quest for something that doesn't exist. The expression in the Master's eyes, when he finally said 'This isn't what I asked you to find ... I am so very sorry,' is still with him.

He walks east, away from the Master's house, away from the slopes where he found the stone, which only ten days earlier he thought of as a sacred place. He feels betrayed. By the stone and by the mountain that yielded it, by the Master who sent him to find it, by God, by destiny ... Tears of profound disillusionment are running down his face. He has failed. He has failed the Master. For many days he walks, just following the road. He walks without seeing or hearing, his senses dulled with pain and hopelessness. He doesn't know what to do next or where to go. He follows the path, meeting very few people along the way and finding just enough to eat and drink to stay alive, even though he doesn't care anymore about staying alive. Finally, his tears dry up.

After twenty-eight days, the landscape is changing. There is more vegetation – shrubs and grasses, trees as well. As he walks on, the landscape becomes greener still, and soon his sharp eyes detect a settlement in the distance. After some time, a long line of palm trees comes into view, and his pace quickens. The village is further away than he thought, but at last he reaches the entrance, where he is welcomed by intense yellow and red flowers turning their heads towards the sun. Only once before, a long time ago, has he seen flowers like these. He squats down to take in their striking beauty. When he straightens, he suddenly feels how thirsty he is, having carefully rationed his water in the past few days – his instinct for survival must still be intact. It is his first act of self-reflection in weeks, and he is aware of its significance. He smiles as he marvels at how strong this instinct must be, because consciously the will to live deserted him after seeing the Master.

He enters the village and follows the path. It is the middle of the afternoon, and there is no one about. Clusters of date palms, a few pines and some other trees are scattered in between simple clay dwellings. There are fruit trees and shrubs with purple-red berries. He continues along the path, and after a few minutes he comes upon a well, in the middle of an open space that must be the village square. He scoops up the clear water with his hands and drinks slowly. It is cool and he savours it. He washes his face and splashes water on the top of his head, letting it trickle down his beard and neck. Closing his eyes, he tilts his head all the way back, breathing deeply. He drinks again. The water tastes sweet, and for the first time since he left the Master he feels gratitude.

A short distance from the well is a pine tree, standing by itself. He has never seen such a huge, splendid tree. It must be very old. He suddenly feels how tired and sore his body is after so many days of walking and little sleep. Without another thought, he walks over to the tree and sits down, his back resting against the trunk. He looks up at the branches. Higher up, some are broken, but the tree is healthy. Its deep roots provide the nourishment it needs. He closes his eyes, blissfully aware of the trunk that is supporting his back both gently and firmly. After a while, he feels his back merging with the tree.

When he opens his eyes, the sun is much lower. To his surprise, he feels refreshed. For the first time since leaving the house of the Master, his head is clear and his body rested. It is as if he has emerged from a sandstorm. The water has washed away the dust and the pain, and the tree has infused him with life. He looks up once more, marvelling at how far up the branches reach and the beautiful pattern they create against the soft blue sky. He moves a little away from the trunk and gently strokes the bark in recognition of its gift to him. Then he gets up and looks around.

He is no longer alone. People are quietly busying themselves around their huts and he hears children's voices calling out. At the well, a woman is struggling to lift a large jar filled to the brim with water. He walks towards her, and she puts the jar down again and smiles warmly.

'Good afternoon, traveller,' she greets him. 'Welcome to our village. I saw you sitting under the tree. It's one of our most honoured trees. I trust it has given you rest and has replenished your strength.'

'Thank you,' he says, inclining his head to her, 'thank you very much.' Her dark hair, greying at the temples, is tied back, drawing attention to her lovely face, which is slightly wrinkled around her mouth and eyes. Her light-green robes reveal the delicate bone structure of her neck.

'It is indeed a remarkable tree, I must say that,' he says in answer. 'When I arrived here earlier this afternoon, the first thing I did was drink from this well – I was so thirsty and the water was delicious – and then it was as if the tree was beckoning me, and I was glad to sit down in its shade and rest my back against its trunk. I have walked for many days, and to tell you the truth, I was very weary. I had a rather … devastating experience, and I think I must have lost touch with myself, with my heart, my soul. I'm not sure how to explain it. However, after being with that tree, it was as if I finally woke up from a long, lonely, frightful dream, and I feel I have come to my senses again. It is as you said, the tree has given me peace and strength. It invited me to lean against its trunk, so that I would receive some of its vitality. It must be hundreds and hundreds of years old. Imagine its wisdom! I fell asleep, and when I woke up, everything seemed different. It's nothing short of miraculous. I feel cleansed and clear and energised. The water too had something to do with it – its coolness, its softness. I can't remember the last time I felt so at peace with myself and everything around me. I am so very grateful.'

It is more than he has spoken to anyone in a long time, and he is surprised by how easy it is to talk to her. It is because she truly listens, he realises. She is listening to his every word, and not only his words. She is completely with him, her eyes steady and relaxed, and once or twice she nods her head almost imperceptibly. When he has finished speaking, she is quiet for a while.

'That's what the tree does for people,' she says with a smile. 'I too and many others have been healed in some way by that tree. I'm so glad it could do the same for you. And you are right, the water here has a special quality. It is infused with compassion.'

'Infused with compassion?' His eyes widen. 'What do you mean? How can that be?' For a moment, he is puzzled, but suddenly he knows it must be true. 'Compassion ... yes, I think I see ... I could feel it, now you mention it, but didn't realise what it was. I just drank and relieved my thirst. I did notice a sense of gratitude, which I hadn't felt for a long time.'

'Yes, that's the best way to receive compassion, to simply take it when it comes to you, in whatever form. You must have had a great need for it. You know, I have lived here all my life, and for me it's normal to drink compassion every day and wash with it and cook with it and clean my hut with it, but from what I gather, that's unusual, and guests are often astounded. It profoundly influences the way we live here in our village. I'm sure you can imagine that. We are very blessed.'

'Do you know how it happened? That the water came to contain compassion, I mean?'

'It's been like that for centuries. We have a story about how our village began. One day, a group of people passed by here. They had been wandering through the desert for many years, on some kind of spiritual quest. It seems they lost their way and couldn't find water. For years, they had been able to navigate well enough, or maybe their Gods guided them in such a way that they were never too far from a water source. This particular time, however, their knowledge of the terrain or the divine powers that had protected them for so long failed them. They had lost many of their group, and all of them would have succumbed if they hadn't stumbled upon this well. It might not have been there very long, or perhaps their Gods manifested it for them then and there – we don't know. The story goes that they wept with gratitude for the life-saving water but at the same time shed tears of profound grief for the loved ones they had lost. Legend has it that their tears contained a very particular ratio of gratitude and sorrow. The essence of those tears has been in our well ever since. When you drink the water, you sense at an unconscious level what they felt at the time, and the subtle energy of the gratitude and sorrow left by their tears is what we experience as compassion.'

He is deeply touched by the story. He has never heard anything like it, yet he knows it must have happened this way. He sees with his mind's eye the people who perished in the desert, many centuries ago. He sees the others, exhausted, drinking the water, sobbing, tearing their hair in grief. He hears them call upon their Gods to have mercy, to bring back their loved ones. Through their terrible misfortune they had imbued the water with unique properties, to the benefit of many who came after them, including himself. In shedding those tears, they had atoned for the loss of their loved ones.

He contemplates all of this. It seems he has come to an extraordinary place – the water, the life-giving tree. He must have had strong guidance to find this oasis, given the state he was in. Or perhaps that's when guidance is most effective, when the mind is too exhausted to think? For the third time that day, he feels profound gratitude, and finally he remembers that life is always as it should be.

'You will need somewhere to sleep,' the woman says. 'Would you like to stay with me? I live alone. My daughter lives with her husband's family, here in the village. My husband died and my son left many years ago. He was only seventeen and wanted to discover what else the world had to offer beyond our trees and our water. I'm still hoping he will find his way back home, but it's been a long time now, and I know that children don't always come back to their parents. The world is such a big, enticing place. Dangerous too, at times. We need to let our children go, that's the nature of things, but I miss him every day … I love him so very much …'

She stops talking and for a while is lost in thought, and he waits respectfully. It suddenly crosses his mind that he too is such a son, and that somewhere, far from here, his mother will die, or maybe has done so already, without ever again setting eyes on the son she loved very much. He hasn't thought of his mother in years, but remembers her gentle presence and endless thoughtfulness. A wave of empathy washes over him as he imagines his mother's sorrow.

'I'm sorry, I know this is difficult to understand if you are not a mother. Don't worry. What I wanted to say … I have enough space and would welcome the company.'

He thanks her and accepts without hesitation. He picks up the water jug and follows her to her hut.

Later, when the woman, who told him her name is Esin, is preparing the evening meal, he sits in front of her hut. A little to one side, there is a tall date palm; to the other, a couple of fig trees – he recognises the smooth, white bark and the distinctive fragrance. Small plants with green, red and purple leaves cover the ground. The palm leaves rustle softly in the breeze from the desert, and small, brightly coloured birds of a kind he has never seen before are chirruping. For a long while he has no thoughts, his senses immersed in the sights, the sounds, the scents and the feel of the cooling breeze against his skin.

He becomes aware of a change in himself. He doesn't know why the Master rejected the Most Magnificent Stone the Earth Could Ever Yield, but he is no longer so terribly upset. He has no idea what to do next, but he knows that something will come along when the time is right, just like this village with its water and the old pine did. All those years of digging and searching cannot have been for nothing, even though the purpose of his quest is far from clear to him. Nonetheless, he knows there must be a purpose, no matter how drawn-out or unimaginable – for life is always as it should be.

It is getting dark when Esin comes towards him, carrying a large dish. With a smile, she places it in the middle of a low, flattened tree stump near the entrance of the hut that is her table. Then she goes inside and returns a moment later with a jug of water and two bowls.

'Are you hungry?' she asks, and she gestures for him to join her at the table. There are generous slices of meat, wedges of green melon, dates, apricots, soft white cheese and flat bread, all beautifully arranged. It has been years since he has seen such an abundance of food on one plate. It smells delicious – it must be the spices she cooked the meat in – and he suddenly is immensely hungry.

'Thank you, thank you so much. I don't know what to say. It looks absolutely wonderful,' he says, hardly able to take his eyes off it. 'You make me feel so welcome, I wish I could thank you properly.'

'It's not often these days that I have a chance to cook for someone else,' she says. 'That in itself is a gift. I enjoy cooking for others. Please, help yourself.'

Following her example, he stuffs some bread with meat and cheese and takes a bite. He doesn't recognise the spices, but the taste is full and rich and the meat is lean and tender. They take their time, eating slowly, aware that this is somehow a special occasion. When they have finished eating, they continue to sit there. The evening has become still. The birds have gone to sleep, and the desert breeze has died down. Apart from the soft light cast by a sliver of moon, it is dark. Esin looks thoughtfully at her guest.

'Would you like to tell me about your journey?' she finally asks. 'About what it was that happened to you and brought you here?'

He sighs, wondering what to answer, but sensing her curiosity and concern, he tells her about the Master and the Blue Stone. How he met the Master when he was hardly more than a boy, and felt an intense urge to learn from him. For years, all he had done was make tea and sweep his house. Being in the Master's presence was enough. One day, the Master told him about a special stone and asked him to find it. He was honoured to be entrusted with what felt like an important task, and he had wandered and searched and dug for more years than he cared to remember. Images of those years flood his mind as he relives his intense desire to find the treasured stone and deliver it to the Master. Finally, he looks up – is Esin still there? She nods encouragingly, and he tells her the whole story: how, not long ago, he finally found the Most Magnificent Stone the Earth Could Ever Yield, and all that happened since.

'The rest you know,' he says with a smile. 'Since I drank from your well and rested against the old pine tree, it is no longer difficult to accept the Master's rejection of what I took to be the ultimate Blue Stone. But not only that. I have felt a deeper kind of peace settle into my heart. I no longer feel driven to wander and search and dig. I'm so glad to be freed, at long last, from the torment of wondering whether I would find the "right" stone – freed, also, from the excitement when I was convinced that I had found it. It's such a relief to be no longer prey to those emotions, which came and went relentlessly, for years and years, just because of what I did or didn't find in the earth. I have no words to describe how peaceful I feel, for the first time since I started looking for stones. The thought comes to me that perhaps it wasn't the Master I was trying to please, but, rather, something inside of me. Yes, maybe that's what it was. All those days when I was walking as if in a dream, and was guided here, I couldn't get the thought out of my head that I had wasted all those years, because I had not been able to bring the Master the stone he wanted me to find. I understand now that spending my life looking for something that doesn't exist has not been a mistake. This is the gift I received today, through drinking the compassion in the water, feeling the life force from the tree, and meeting you – because you listened to me and helped me find the way back to myself. On top of that, you prepared a meal that, apart from being heartening and nourishing and sweet, which I very much needed, contained love and care of a kind I hadn't felt since I left the house of my mother. I thank you from the bottom of my heart.'

Esin casts down her eyes in acknowledgement. 'It's my very great pleasure. I trust you know that.' He looks at her and nods. Neither of them speaks for a long time. Then Esin breaks the silence.

'You can stay here for as long as you like. In fact, I hope you will stay for a while. I'm wondering, though. About four or five days away lives someone you might like to meet. When you were talking about the Master, I was reminded of him. He must be old by now, I suppose, but I have a feeling he is still in the same spot, close to the river. If you continue eastwards and a little to the north, you will notice that everything is greener. There once was a river in this area, but it has gone underground. The water that wells up here in our village is ancient groundwater. Just one day from here, the river comes to the surface and becomes a real river, eventually flowing into the sea, although that's still very far away. The old man I mentioned is known as the Sage, and people used to pass here on their way to see him. He might still be there, and maybe you will find it helpful to talk to him.'

'Really?' he says, his mouth falling open. 'Are you sure, just four or five days away? It would be absolutely wonderful if he were still there and I could go and see him. Esin, it's incredible that I met you, that you were fetching water when you did! Yes, I would very much like to go and see this Sage, but for now I will accept your kind offer and stay here for a few days – drink the water and spend some more time with the tree.'

'That sounds like a good idea,' she says. 'Regain your strength first. There's no rush. We have been talking for a long time. It's late, and you must be tired. Let's go inside and I'll show you where you can sleep.' She takes the empty dish and leads the way inside. He follows with the water jug and the bowls and they put them on a shelf in a corner of the hut. Then she shows him an alcove. 'Here's your bed, I trust you will be comfortable enough. My son used to sleep here. I hope you will have a good night.'

All of a sudden, he feels how tired he is. 'Thank you, thank you again for everything, and a good night to you too.'

She leaves him, and he takes off his footwear and some of his clothes and lies down on the bed. He covers himself with a blanket – the nights are cool. For a while he listens to her pottering about, enjoying the everyday sounds of human company, then he falls into a deep, restful sleep.

During the days that follow, he spends many hours sitting underneath the tree, the bark touching his back. It is easy to open himself and let the tree's energy saturate every part of him. After only a few days, his body feels stronger and thoroughly alive, his mind clear like the water from the well and his heart soaked in acceptance and gratitude. He is deeply appreciative of this profound transformation, aware that he has entered a new stage of his life. On the evening of the fifth day, he tells Esin that he will leave the next morning to find the Sage. She nods and smiles.

'I am glad,' is all she says. And then, after a while: 'If ever you meet someone who is travelling in this direction, please tell them to come and see me and give me some news of you.'

'I will,' he says, 'of course.'

He sleeps one last night in the alcove in her hut, which has become more like home than anything he has known since childhood, and gets up at first light. Esin gives him water, fresh bread, dates and almonds for the journey and accompanies him to the edge of the village.

'It's an easy walk,' she says, 'you'll see. Just keep heading east. At the end of today, you will get to the point where the river comes above ground. It's a magical place. You could spend the night there, and watch the sunrise if you can, it's magnificent. The river will be just a trickle at first, but you'll see it right away, and soon after it gets wider. Don't cross it. All you need to do is follow it for another three or four days. That will take you quite close to where I think the Sage lives. It's near a settlement. Someone will know if he is still there and where exactly you can find him.'

One last time he looks into her gentle, intelligent eyes. He has grown fond of her. 'Thank you, Esin! I will never forget you and all that you've done for me. Words cannot express how thankful I am, but I know that you know. Be well.'

She nods, returning his gaze. 'Yes, I know. It was so very good meeting you. Thank you, too. Good travels and take care!'

She watches him disappear into the distance, then slowly walks back into the village.

He walks eastward with a spring in his step, aware that he couldn't feel more different from the day he arrived in the village, only six days earlier. As Esin said, the walk is easy. At the end of the day, he reaches the source of the river, where he spends the night and watches the sunrise the next morning. It is indeed spectacular, a huge, red ball rising majestically over the river, staining the sky with innumerable shades of pink, red and gold that are reflected in the water. The rest of his journey is uneventful, and in the morning of the fifth day he reaches the hut of the Sage Esin told him about.

Ian stopped talking and we waited. It felt like when an episode of a Netflix series finishes at some crucial point in the story, except that with Netflix I would reach for the remote and click on the next episode to keep watching, until deep into the night if need be. It seemed we weren't going to get another episode tonight. We would have to wait for at least another week. I felt a sudden panic when it crossed my mind that we might never know if the Seeker for Stones met the Sage, or what it was they spoke about, because sometimes our spirit-visitors left us with an unfinished story. The first time this happened I felt utterly indignant, like a child denied a promised lollipop, something that had actually happened to me as a four-year-old at a Punch and Judy show. I had screamed at the injustice of it until my parents provided me with a lollipop from another source. At our Thursday night gatherings, I occasionally felt let down by a story-teller. Sometimes, a story was abandoned because of Ian's state of mind, but it could also be that other matters were considered more relevant for the group as a whole, and the topic was changed for that reason. I had to do some work in those cases, in order to let go of the people who, in the course of a story, had become dear to me.

'I am sorry, we will have to stop here,' the evening's narrator said, 'but we do have time for some questions, if you like.'

I jumped in without considering anyone. 'Are we going to hear the rest next week? Please?'

Ian leaned to his left where I was sitting, making me feel conspicuous. 'We cannot see the future with such precision,' he said, with a big smile. 'We don't work with weeks where we are, but you know that by now.' He laughed a big belly laugh. 'Don't worry, we're only teasing you. We understand the urgency you feel about the meeting between the Seeker for Stones and the Sage, and you are right to feel that urgency.'

It was enough to reassure me, but it left me thinking that it would be a while before I would ask something again. I didn't enjoy being the centre of attention in such a way.

'Their meeting was highly significant,' he continued, 'a culmination of their lives. Their coming together was strongly guided and would affect many. We have every intention to tell you about it, next week if you will, as long as your medium makes sure he is in good shape. He should eat well, get enough sleep, and not be involved in too much of the drama that is never far away in your dimension.'

I wondered why on earth he would say such a thing, but after the session Ian explained that he had been rather taken up by a dispute with his neighbours about some trees on the boundary of their properties. They thought they were too big, and wanted them removed. I knew Ian as someone who kept his cool in just about any situation, but the threatened removal of mature, healthy trees would be the sort of thing to deeply upset him.

'The same is true for you all,' our visitor continued. 'Try not to get too bogged down by what happens in your everyday lives. I know that for some of you that's easier said than done. Don't force yourselves. There is never any point in suppressing or ignoring challenging feelings. They are a normal, necessary part of life, for the spiritually advanced too.' He laughed again, and I couldn't suppress a smile. It flashed through my mind that he was the guide who once had taken on the identity of the Old Man with a Twinkle in his Eye. There must be a deep-seated streak of playful mischievousness in the make-up of this soul. However, when he resumed he was again serious.

'At the same time, be philosophical about your own and others' emotional reactions, and remember that, like anything else, they will pass. We would like you to be here with a certain level of serenity next time, when we will tell you more about the Blue Stone, and even, perhaps, how you can find yours.'

This was much more than I had bargained for, and everyone was quiet. Finally, Jason cleared his throat and asked in a small voice if he would be allowed to ask something he was really curious about.

'Certainly,' came the answer immediately. Our guest sounded cheerful. 'There is a very obvious question most of you would like to ask, but you don't dare because of what I just told you. You are concerned about being greedy, ha-ha. Don't worry! It is your birthright to be curious. Please go ahead!'

'The water,' Jason said. 'The compassion in the water.' He described an article he had recently read. Bowls of water were exposed to groups of people who had generated positive feelings, like gratitude or appreciation. Other bowls of water from the same source were subjected to feelings of shame or anger. Then the water was frozen. The water that had been exposed to the positive vibes showed beautiful, intricate, symmetrical crystals. The crystals in the other water didn't have any symmetry and the patterns were random. 'Some scientists said it was all nonsense,' Jason finished, 'but something similar seems to have happened in the story. Could you please tell us more about it?'

Ian's head nodded. 'Yes, yes, that was a very interesting experiment indeed! Don't forget that all is energy. If you can truly see that – or accept that – it makes sense: if water is energy, and thoughts and feelings are energy, and you bring those together, it is likely that the energies will influence each other. There are still many scientists who do not appreciate all the implications of this discovery – that all is energy, I mean – as it upsets some of the main principles that have formed the foundation of their methodology and philosophy in recent history. Attitudes are changing, however, and a new generation of researchers is emerging who are open to radically new findings, even if these don't always fit within the old parameters. They are less afraid to trust their intuition and more confident because of it. Their outlook allows them to be more creative, which makes them freer than researchers who still mainly operate through the rational mind and follow strict protocols. For a long time, science has largely been a method of description, its goal to find or establish patterns that allow the unknown to be described in terms of the known. It often has the strange notion, for example, that experiments need to be reproducible so that they can be used to predict outcomes. It might be useful to be able to predict an earthquake, but, mostly, life isn't about predictability, even though the wish to have some kind of control of your environment is understandable and usually well-intended. In reality, everything only ever happens once, in its own unique present moment. Life's main purpose is creative exploration, as we keep telling you, and the essence of exploring is that you don't know what you are going to find. It's best to travel with a mind that's truly open to what might lie beyond what is known. The mind-set of traditional science keeps you trapped in a kind of closed circuit that leaves little room for any genuinely new discoveries. The old parameters in science have been useful, but a new approach is imminent and necessary.

'We know that you have a special interest in this matter of a better working-relationship between science and spirituality. We have come across something similar a little while ago, haven't we? It was about the connection of the heart and the brain then, and we concluded that it was crucial to topple the mind off its position of dominance, in order for the voice of the heart to become audible. It's much more reliable and will open up myriad possibilities. You have so much to look forward to! Your technology helps people share their findings with many others everywhere on your planet. It's only a matter of time until mainstream scientific thinking will gradually merge with another paradigm, something that does more justice to the whole mysterious phenomenon of life and the much wider perspectives that are being discovered all the time. A few generations ago, you had a scientist who famously said that intuition is "a sacred gift" and the rational mind "a faithful servant". We are not even sure that the mind is always faithful, by the way, but this man had much integrity. He was a precursor and intuited something vitally important. It happens often, as part of momentum towards big change, that there are people with a kind of sixth sense – as you would call it – for developments that are on the threshold but will stay out of reach of mainstream thinking for a while longer. Their enlightened thoughts and ideas appear briefly, and then go underground again, a bit like the river in the story. It sprang up in the village in the form of a well and went back underground to resurface much further along.

'Which brings us back to your question about the compassion in the water. It's exactly as you heard in the story. The tears of the people who drank from the well contained a very specific mix of gratitude and sorrow. It was a unique coming-together of crucial elements that cannot be recreated – it is impossible to make people shed similar tears, or to reproduce them using technology. The tears themselves evaporated quickly, but their essence remained and left a kind of imprint, which was taken on by the water welling up from the ground in that spot. Your healing art of homeopathy works on a similar principle, in the sense that the energy of a substance is more potent than the substance itself. Water has memory. Did you know that? It's something that is on the brink of being rediscovered in your world by some forward-thinking scientists. The compassion stayed in the well in the village. The water of the river that the Seeker for Stones reached at the end of the story was pure and delicious and central to the lives of the people who lived in its vicinity, but it didn't contain compassion.'

'That group of people,' said Sonia softly, 'were they…?'

'Yes, they were the group you have heard about earlier, who were led by Sarwhar on their quest for Great Unity. It happened several years after the events we told you about. They were tired and discouraged by then, because they never found even the smallest trace of what they thought of as Great Unity. Sarwhar was among the survivors. Their getting lost was an overt sign of his having lost the way to his heart. The compassion in the water eventually brought him back to his conscience and made him see the grave errors of his single-minded leadership. He was shocked to the core, declined to be leader any longer, and left it to others to decide what to do next. It was a very tough lesson. Together, they built a small settlement around the well and started a new life there. With time, others settled there too and the village grew. The story you've just heard, about Esin and the Seeker for Stones, took place nearly a thousand years later.'

'That's how potent that compassion-mix was?' asked Jason. 'It was still there after all that time?'

'Yes, those kinds of memories are long-lasting. Centuries later, there were wars, and the village was destroyed, and I doubt that anyone would be able to find the exact location of it anymore. It all happened a very long time ago by your standards, but, provided that there is no contamination of any kind, anyone digging in the right place would find that the water still contains compassion.'

'Couldn't you give a rough indication?' We understood that Jason was really serious about this and ready to go anywhere in the world to start digging. 'Was it the Middle East? Egypt? Afghanistan?'

Our guest of the evening laughed. 'I'm sorry, I have no idea, and, anyway, it doesn't seem the most effective approach to increase compassion in your world. There are easier ways. Actually, you only need to travel as far as your own heart, and you will find all the compassion you need. We'll talk about it soon, perhaps next week, when we hope to continue the story, at the express request of your friend over there.'

All heads turned towards me, but I only vaguely noticed. I was amazed at the compassion imprinted in the water, and shocked at what had happened to Sarwhar's group in the end. I was also oddly relieved that Sarwhar had survived and that Nila and Baddar and the others had left when they did. That's what I meant when I mentioned I often find it hard to let go of people, even in stories or movies. Before I met Fred, I had a boyfriend who used to get annoyed about this – he was the jealous kind, I discovered later, and he never liked it when he didn't have my undivided attention. 'You shouldn't care so much,' he would say, 'let people go, they'll be all right. And if they're not, it's their problem, their life. You have too much attachment.' 'Attachment' was his pet subject, along with 'unconditional love'.

'Could I ask something?' I forgot all about not wanting to ask another question. Suddenly, I urgently wanted to understand this. 'Could you talk about attachment, please? Is it always bad?'

Our guest laughed. 'Bad? Of course it isn't! But it's true that some people make it so. It all depends. Without a doubt, unhealthy attachments exist, and in those cases it's best to learn to let go. However, there can be other issues at play that people think of as attachment, but in reality have to do with their fear of emotional intimacy. Some people easily feel beholden. So, you see, this whole matter of attachment is not black and white. Psychologists have written countless books on the subject, and among some spiritual teachers it's a hot topic, so to speak. If you find it interesting, by all means read up on it. As far as we're concerned, it's not an issue. In reality, everything is One, remember? There is nothing to attach to or detach from. Attachment and detachment are concepts, they aren't real, and when people are too preoccupied with them, it's usually because they aren't able to trust their hearts.

'As we've already announced to our friend who wants to go digging for compassion in Afghanistan, we will talk about the heart and its central role sometime soon. Fear of attachment often stands in the way of compassion. Once you are comfortable in your heart, you won't worry anymore about whether something qualifies as love or attachment or whatever words you can think of. All of these cause more separation, no matter what theories your minds invent to the contrary. When you live in your heart, you simply connect to whoever is there at that moment, and are loving and compassionate without further thought. It will be effortless, I assure you. Please don't be afraid to love.'

COMPASSION SPEAKS

We start to feel our common ground

Charles had been late for babysitting, and I was the last to arrive the following Thursday, right on the dot of eight. I took off my shoes, slipped in quickly, and sat down next to Elspeth, who had kept me a chair. Normally, people would be talking among themselves until Ian greeted us, a sign he was ready to begin. Tonight, however, there wasn't a sound to be heard. The lights were dimmed more than usual, giving prominence to the flames of two big candles that flanked a large grey-stone jar of white hydrangeas in a corner of the studio. I settled down quickly, not wanting to disturb any more than I already had. We sat like this for quite a while. Then Ian spoke.

'I'd like you to be very quiet, please. I'm not sure what it is, but tonight feels different, and I need you all to be as silent as you can. I really mean your thoughts. Please quieten your thoughts.'

I felt Elspeth next to me take a deep breath and followed her example. I visualised a dark sky, with a few stars here and there to give depth to my picture. I was pulled into this endless space and immediately felt myself spreading, becoming less substantial. Everyone must have gone through their own ritual of quieting their minds, and the atmosphere in the room changed noticeably. Why didn't we do this more often, I wondered? The stillness felt so good. Then this thought too disappeared into my boundless space.

'I feel someone here,' said Ian, when it was sufficiently silent for him. 'I'm not sure who it is, and I have a feeling he or she isn't going to reveal it.' He closed his eyes, took a few breaths and started talking. I wasn't sure if I imagined it, but his voice seemed a little deeper and perhaps had more resonance than usual.

'Good evening! I will reveal who I am, but your medium is right, this is a slightly different process. I am Compassion, Compassion Personified, if you like. Our communication will be smoother, more convivial too, if you remember that I am not far from you. In fact, I live inside your heart. I am you. All of Consciousness is energy. The energy that is you on the earthly plane is denser than ours, slower – I think you know that – but that's the only difference. In essence, we are all made of the same stuff. Please keep this in mind when we converse with you.

'Last time, you heard how the water from the well came to contain compassion through a particular mix of grief and gratitude. Grief is a primordial emotion, the first emotion experienced by human beings when they started thinking of themselves as separate from their Source. It exists on the same continuum as gratitude, if you can imagine that, with grief at one end and gratitude at the other and all their shades and gradations in between. One is about lack through loss, the other about a sense of fullness and abundance. Grief occurs when love that is felt deeply can no longer be expressed, be it through physical death or other circumstances that keep people apart. Ultimately, love can always flow, across continents or disagreements, and even across what you think of as death, but as you are living in physicality, you will naturally want to experience love in ways that allow you to express that physicality. That is how it is intended. You would like to feel someone's physical warmth, give them a hug, for example, or make love. You want to have that sense of connection by looking someone in the eyes or hearing the timbre of their voice as they talk to you. Even preparing a meal, like Esin did for her seeker-visitor, can be a profound expression of love. When you love a spouse or child or parent or friend like this, you feel intense grief when you are no longer able to express your love in this manner. Your love has nowhere to go, and you feel as if you will drown in this excess of love that stagnates in big pools everywhere in your body. As long as someone is alive, somewhere on the planet, you can still hope that one day you will be able to be with them in a way that enables you to love them as your heart desires – that was the hope Esin still had, for example, about her son, even though it was waning – but when someone leaves you through death, most of you experience it as a definite parting, and this is why the death of a loved one is usually the most profound source of grief.

'This is what happened in the story of the well you heard last week. There was loss of life, leading to the deepest feelings of grief, but there also was life regained upon finding the well, which gave rise to profound gratitude. To feel both extremes of the continuum so acutely at the same time is very, very unusual. Maybe you can picture it like this: both ends of the line that is the continuum had become so heavy that the line was bent, as it were, and then they touched each other, forming a circle. This caused a kind of short-circuiting, resulting in the energy of compassion being released. It is interesting that in some ancient, esoteric sects, the symbol for compassion is a circle. Compassion is a first step towards healing the sense of separation that you experience so strongly here on your planet, and the circle represents this making-whole.

'It is not only in matters of life and death, however, that compassion is essential in lessening the existential pain of separation. There is a great, constant need for compassion in the lives of just about everyone on your planet, because of its power to lead you straight into your heart, where you can sense your interconnectedness with all other forms of being, Oneness, if you like. To the rational mind, Oneness makes little sense, as your senses clearly tell you that you are all separate beings. The mind analyses, pulls apart. The heart allows and doesn't feel conflict.

'It is in the mind that language resides, however, and this is why words can cause separation. They have a tendency to force you into your head if you are not careful. Definitions only serve a narrow purpose, and if you truly want to understand what someone is trying to tell you, it's usually best not to have too many preconceived ideas. As a society, you have largely lost the art of listening – simply being present with an open mind, without offering solutions or even thinking you know anything at all. When you listen to someone, their words can lead you into their heart, which at the same time leads you into your own heart. And when you are both there, you are on common ground as it were, and everything becomes easier. This is why, in evolved societies of the past, the present and the future, people listen to each other until there is consensus. The aim of having a discussion is not to establish who is right or what would be best for the majority, but to reach a place of deep mutual understanding.

'Confrontations between people are never personal, as you have seen in our stories. With your disputes and disagreements, you simply give each other a chance to become aware of the false beliefs that obscure your view. Once you understand this mechanism, even forgiveness is no longer necessary. For what is there to forgive when you can see someone as playing a crucial role in alerting you to something you need to see? However, such experiences can leave emotional residue in their wake, and then forgiveness helps to seal the healing between you.

'Because I have the honour of speaking to you as Compassion Personified on this occasion, I would like to encourage you to explore the compassion in your heart. There is no need to go on a quest to find it in far-away lands,' he smiled in Jason's direction, 'even though we appreciate your feelings. As we said, it's the very stuff you are made of.

'If you like, if any of you has a question perhaps, we would be delighted to talk with you a little longer.'

'Thank you, yes, I have a question, if I may,' said Ralph. 'I like what you said about exploring compassion. Could you please explain how I could learn to do that?'

'Sure, yes, thank you for that question, it's something that matters for everyone. We will do an exercise together.' As soon as he said this, we all started moving in our chairs. He waited patiently until we were settled. 'I understand,' he smiled. 'When you have a body, it must feel comfortable, mustn't it? So, when you are ready ... close your eyes, please. Zoom in on the centre of your chest, and feel your heart. Notice your breath. Notice your chest slowly rising and falling ... Now, tune into a scenario ... a memory, an image, a fantasy that fills you with gratitude or appreciation or compassion. Or you could simply focus on the sound of one of those words. It really doesn't matter. Pick the word or feeling that resonates with you. Be creative, and don't worry too much about getting it right. Don't forget that intention itself is a powerful energy, and that in your essence you are a loving, compassionate being.'

At first, I struggled a bit, wondering about 'the centre of your chest'. Wasn't the heart a bit to the left? Or was this another kind of heart? I was annoyed with myself and my literal-mindedness. But when he mentioned the power of intention, I relaxed, and suddenly I felt solid and secure and wonderfully peaceful. It was easy.

Compassion Personified left us to it.

'You see?' he resumed after a little while. 'Even just three or four minutes is enough. Feelings of grief or sadness also take you to your heart, but if you would like to move into your heart consciously, we recommend compassion or gratitude for obvious reasons. However, often it is impossible to separate out those feelings completely. You have probably had the experience of feeling profoundly thankful for something, let's say passing an exam that was important for you, whilst at the same time being sad for others who failed it. Or of being appreciative of a special meal and suddenly being struck by the thought that many people on your planet are hungry. Everything is mixed together, nothing is separate.'

Ralph nodded vehemently. 'Thank you, thank you very much.' He was completely engrossed, his eyes focused. When he spoke again, there was hesitation in his voice. 'But, um … how did you know that, about my exam? Except, it wasn't quite like that, you know. I did a course in electro-technique earlier this year, and I was the only one in the class who didn't pass the exam. I felt so bad about spoiling the party. The core of what you said was true, though, because the others were sad on my behalf. Some of them have helped me revise everything since, and they've been pushing me to take the exam again. They made me see that I could actually be quite good at this. It's just that I'm not used to doing exams, you see, and I suppose I wasn't very confident. Their response when they found out that I hadn't passed was really compassionate. So many good things have come from it, not least the friendships I now have.'

Our guest smiled. 'We are very glad you shared this story. It's a good illustration of what we were trying to explain. Thank you! But we didn't know about your exam. We must have picked it up as it was floating from your mind. It illustrates that thought is energy, like everything else. We apologise if we are repetitive, but it's part of the main lesson: the nature of everything is energy, and you can't hear it often enough. There won't be any exams on it, though, and we are sure that you will gradually start having experiences that show you this is true. We agree with your new friends, by the way, that you could be very good at the subject you are studying, and would like to take this opportunity to encourage you to continue in this field.'

'Thank you, I so much appreciate this. I certainly will continue my studies. What you say means a lot to me. Thank you again.'

I had never seen Ralph so engaged. I didn't know much about him – even though he had been in the group for years – except that he lived by himself in an apartment somewhere in town. He was in his forties, stocky and round-faced with blue eyes that were lovely, now I came to think of it, open and honest and alert. He was blond, and sported a number 2 haircut, just like Colin. I had often judged his questions as unintelligent and suddenly realised I had done him an injustice. It would be more accurate to say that he was much less self-conscious and less afraid to be himself than the rest of us. He had a different background, perhaps, but by now I should have known that having an education or not was of no consequence in the greater scheme of things. He never came along when we went for drinks after a session, and I suddenly realised that we had never asked him. I hadn't known anything about his studies, let alone his failing the exam. I felt ashamed. What was the point of learning about all of this if it didn't make us look out for each other?

In the meantime, Elspeth had put up her hand. Ian invited her to go ahead.

'I would like to thank you, Ralph,' Elspeth started, her eyes shining with tears. 'I admire your perseverance and wish you all the best when you take the exam. I'm sure I speak on behalf of all of us.' She looked around and we all nodded and smiled at Ralph and her. 'Thank you for asking that question,' she went on, 'and for telling us how the other people on your course helped you believe in yourself.'

Quiet tears rolled down her face as Ralph whispered 'Thank you' to her.

'Could I ask something?' Elspeth said when the tears had stopped.

'Yes, of course, please do.'

'It's about my tears. Not just now, but in general. It happens so easily. I don't mind so much here, but usually people don't understand and it embarrasses me. It can be really awkward.'

'Is it that you feel your heart is nearly too open at times?'

'Yes indeed, that's exactly what it feels like. So open that it almost hurts. All kinds of things bring me to tears. I identify so much with the other person and feel their feelings so acutely that I have little defence. As much as I want to learn about compassion, I need to find a way to be more balanced. At times, it's almost debilitating.'

'We understand. Don't worry, though. As we see it, you are very much on track, and we agree with you that it's a matter of balance. It's true that open-heartedness leads to greater sensitivity, but that doesn't need to be a problem. In our respectful view, a lack of sensitivity is much more problematic. Your world is exposed to relentless noise, and on a daily basis you are inundated with images and stories of violence and suffering. Your days are so crammed full that there is little opportunity to digest the impressions that keep coming your way without let-up. In order to keep a level of sanity, most people respond by switching off. Many have become desensitised, so much so that a certain level of insensitivity has become the norm. As a result, psychologists diagnose the ones who haven't managed to make the shift as "highly sensitive persons", HSPs, a terminology which has connotations of pathology or at least abnormality. The practice of diagnosing people as feeling too deeply and labelling them in a way that indicates they aren't quite normal is not helpful, and doesn't do them justice. Being sensitive is not a condition, it's simply a phase in the process of spiritual growth. There is a strong tendency to want to rationalise emotions in your world, as this gives the illusion of being in control. Emotions are too messy to be neatly categorised in ways that satisfy your slightly misnamed Human Sciences – they don't fit statistics. Once humanity decides it is ready for the next stage of its evolution, all of this will change.

'In the meantime, as your heart starts opening, you might indeed find that you are more easily moved to tears. Try not to mind too much, even if it's inconvenient. Some people cultivate a kind of artificial detachment, in order to protect themselves. We can see how this can be a good strategy in emergencies or when you are working in conditions where you are exposed to high levels of anguish or upset. The bottom line is always to find a way that allows you to function in such circumstances. However, in the case of the normal suffering that is an inherent part of life on Earth, we recommend that you do not shield your heart any more than strictly necessary. Eventually, your feelings will integrate, and it will become easier. Tears that come from feeling deeply – tears of compassion, in fact – are a sign that the membrane between your essence and your worldly persona is thinning and that you are getting closer to your true nature.'

Compassion Personified paused. I felt for Elspeth and admired her courage to share this with the group. It was true that sensitivity was an asset that was not always recognised as such, putting the onus on sensitive people to explain or excuse themselves.

After a while, I remembered the Seeker for Stones. Had he met the Sage? Had Ian not been able to do what they said last time? And I had been late. Had I been too rushed? They had promised we would hear the rest of the story, hadn't they?

'I know,' said our guest, 'that we haven't quite done what we promised. Or, at least, that this might be the feeling some of you have.' Once more, I resorted to staring at the carpet. 'There will be a continuation, and I think it will satisfy your curiosity about what happened when the Sage and the Seeker for Stones met. You have our promise that we will tell you all about it.' He laughed. 'For now, please let it not distract you from what you have just heard. All of what we tell you is related and connected, nothing is arbitrary. Be patient another week, or two or three perhaps.' I could almost feel him winking at me and bit my lip to hide a smile. 'In the end, all will be revealed.'

PORTALS OF THE HEART

We are shown the way

There was an undeniable atmosphere of anticipation that evening. We were all there well before eight, and no one seemed interested in catching up with their neighbour, mindful of the request to be serene. Not that this word described our state very well, but we all did our best, and when Ian came in, the room was quiet. He greeted us with a knowing smile, sat down, softly said hello and closed his eyes.

'I have a feeling,' he said a moment later, 'that there's more than one being who would like to speak to us tonight. I think I feel two different energies. This has never happened before, and it's not possible for me to accommodate more than one entity at a time. I'm sure our guests know this. I will let myself be guided by them, alternate between them maybe, as they see fit. There might be gaps here and there, but that doesn't necessarily matter. I'm not sure how it will happen, but I'm happy to trust the process. I suggest you do too.'

We all nodded earnestly. Not for the first time, I admired Ian's willingness to let others take over his vocal chords. Then Ian started to speak. Someone had arrived.

'When you last heard from me, I was on my way to meet the Sage Esin had told me about. For you, that was a few weeks ago, if I'm not mistaken, for me, a small slice of Eternity.' He laughed. 'It never ceases to be fascinating, this phenomenon of time, does it? I'm aware that you are curious to hear what happened when the Seeker for Stones finally arrived at the hut of the Sage – what it was like when the two of us finally found ourselves face to face. I must start, though, with telling you that it was good for me to walk for a while after I had said goodbye to Esin. It's true that I felt utterly changed after my stay in her village, but I needed those extra days by myself to quietly contemplate all that had happened in such a short time. Walking along the river helped me with that. Water is flow and flexibility, and I wanted to feel those qualities in myself as much as I could. It had been a profound transformation, which had started when I drank from the well in Esin's village. Or earlier maybe, when the Master rejected my stone. Or possibly even before that, when a ray of sunlight revealed the stone to me, and the mountain let me take it. Can you see how everything is connected and that it's impossible to determine cause and effect? My parents too played a role, by allowing me to leave their house to live with the Master at a young age, so I might fulfil my ardent desire – for truth, for beauty, depth … I'm not sure what to call it exactly – and even their parents, who brought them up to be open-minded and generous. There is no beginning and no end; it is the movement of life, fleeting and intangible and at the same time very real. So, I was grateful for those calm, beautiful days when I followed the path along the river on my way to the Sage.'

Ian stopped, slumped a little and was very still. It took no more than a minute, if that, for another visitor to make himself known. Would we finally meet the Sage, I wondered?

'I saw him approach my hut and stop when he noticed me in the doorway. I recognised him immediately. Gladness filled my heart. We had missed each other narrowly in another life, but in this life, as a Sage, my last, I had the great advantage of remembering my soul history and the agreement he and I had made. I knew we wouldn't miss each other again, thanks to Esin – or Nila, if you like. Maybe you sensed that these two soul-expressions have a similar feel. Names aren't so important – you might remember Nila explaining that. She and I, in varying roles and genders, have supported each other across lifetimes in all kinds of ways. This time, she was instrumental in bringing me together with the soul who had been searching for blue stones. Together, he and I were to safeguard the teachings of The Four Portals of the Heart and make sure this knowledge would be passed on. I will tell you about The Portals a little later. First, I'd like to share with you that moment when we met, so you will see how close our connection was and how precious our friendship.

'All my life, I had been looking forward to this moment, and as he was slowly walking towards me, we held each other's gaze. I saw immediately that he was a different person. With this, I don't mean the identity he had adopted to live life on Earth, something we all must do every time. What was significant was that after all those lives of seeking, be it a glistening mountain peak or the secrets of the universe or the Most Magnificent Stone the Earth could Ever Yield, he finally knew there was no need to seek any further. Drinking from the well of compassion and meeting Esin, with whom he also had a deep soul connection, as you might understand, had made the long process of overcoming this major block come to an end. When I saw him approach, I knew he had completed a fundamental life-lesson that had spurred him on for aeons, and that he had done so convincingly, literally not leaving a stone unturned. His life as Seeker for Stones was a metaphor for the thoroughness with which he had accepted his soul journey and brought it to completion. All of this was cause for celebration. We embraced. The mutual recognition was instant. I can't describe the intense joy of reconnecting with a soul-brother on Earth. Nothing, not the highest wisdom or the deepest knowledge, can ever come anywhere near the feeling of a long, warm embrace between two human beings who are coming home to each other. We just stood there, gazing at each other with tears in our eyes, holding each other tightly then letting go and smiling broadly. Everything else had stopped existing. Neither of us said anything, and no words would have done justice to our profound gratitude to have found each other again. It was enough to be in each other's presence, knowing we would speak all we wanted later.

'The following day was spent largely in silence too. He fetched water from the river, and we prepared some food. We sat down in front of my hut, which was close to the river bank. I had built it many years earlier, when I still had the strength of a younger man. I had chosen the site carefully to be as close to the river as possible, taking into account that during part of the year it would be much wider than in other seasons. We sat there for many hours that day, watching the water flow by and listening to its murmur. I encouraged him to take a stroll, as I used to do. I myself couldn't walk much anymore. I think you have understood that I was a very old man by then. Towards the end of the third day, when we were comfortably installed in the dappled shade in front of my hut, I asked him about his adventures and what it was that had happened in order for us to fulfil our shared destiny.

'For a long while, he stared into the water, but then he started to speak, a little hesitantly in the beginning but soon he was taken along by his own narrative. He told me of living with the Master and the many years of searching and digging for blue stones. Of his love for the Master and his deep desire to please him, and his desolation when he learnt that the Most Magnificent Stone the Earth Could Ever Yield had not been what the Master intended him to find. He recounted his feeling that he had failed the Master and how unbearable this had been. He spoke of his profound hopelessness during his long, seemingly aimless walk, and how his strength had been restored so unexpectedly through the water and the tree and the care of Esin – of how good it had been to talk to her, and how she had cooked nourishing meals and let him sleep in the bed that once belonged to her son. And lastly, how she had told him about me, an old, wise man living a few days' walk downstream from the village. At this point, my heart overflowed with thankfulness for Esin, for her dedication to serve in small ways. People don't always realise that these kinds of contributions are crucial, and that vital outcomes are always preceded by the subtle, thoughtful deeds of beings like Esin. "Ever since I drank from the water and rested underneath that mighty tree, I have experienced a tranquillity like never before," my friend the Seeker for Stones concluded. "But there's one thing I'd very much like to know, and it would be wonderful if you could give me the answer: what was it that the Master meant for me to find?"'

Ian was quiet for rather a long time. We looked at him with some concern, and, very briefly, I had another Netflix moment. I had been so captivated by the meeting between these two charismatic spirit-beings that I forgot that a new skill was being asked of Ian – the transition had been so quick the first time. We waited in silence, and, soon, one of them was back.

'Our apologies, it wasn't our intention to add suspense, but we felt it was better that I would tell you from my perspective what the Sage said to me in answer to my question. After all, it was my process and a decisive part of my soul-learning. The Sage had completed his. He only ever had very little to learn from living on Earth, and the few times he came, it was as a service to others.

'When I asked him what it was that the Master had meant for me to find, if not the unique Blue Stone I brought him, he nodded and smiled. "Yes indeed, that is the most important question for you to ask." He looked at me kindly, and suddenly I felt there was nothing about me that he didn't know or couldn't see. It was the most extraordinary gift anyone could have given me, this sense of being known in the deepest parts of my being. I had the realisation that who I was, was all I had ever been required to be. After all those lives of trying to reach the best or the biggest or the highest, I suddenly understood that I was the Most Magnificent Stone the Earth Could Ever Yield. How come it had taken me so long to see it? With that look, he set me forever free from the illusion that I am separate from Source, separate from divinity. Nothing else was needed after that. Yet what he subsequently said was amazing and gave me a much bigger picture of what it meant to be me.'

> 'Before I can answer your question,' the Sage started, 'I have to digress a bit and tell you about how humankind came to live here on this planet. A very long time ago – before time existed, really, for it was long before the first humans arrived on Earth – there was Consciousness. It was everywhere, without end, undivided. Consciousness was never created. It always was. Everything else was projected forth from that initial unity, which is the Source of All That Is and the only constant Truth. All other truths change when the viewpoint changes. At that stage of evolution, there was only one point to view things from. There was no duality. Oneness was all that was known.
>
> 'Then it happened that pockets of Consciousness became, let's say, curious. They wanted to know what else they could be besides Oneness. At first, this was only a thought, and as such it started its creative exploration. We told you how thought is a strong creative power, most particularly in that realm – a single thought of anything at all, and it exists. For a long time, it was a matter of happy experimenting, and all was well. Finally, the most adventurous parts of Consciousness started

their forays into physicality, experimenting with the idea of a separate "I". It was intended to be temporary, and they still felt a firm connection with the collective pool of Consciousness. The plan was to re-join. However, very gradually, something resembling a body was created. The first bodies were a bit ghost-like, not made of flesh and blood like yours. In these translucent forms, they could come and go as they pleased to explore the idea of physicality even further, but never was it assumed that who they were was limited to those forms – they just wanted to experience what it might be like to live in a body. They were particularly intrigued by the intensity of feeling, which they found exhilarating. At that experimenting stage, those feelings were always joyous, and there was a total absence of fear. In the end, though, their investigations led them to lose their way utterly and completely, and so they became human beings in physical bodies.

'The reality of being separate from the whole brought circumstances they had never imagined. The hardest, totally unforeseen part was that they started to feel divided, mainly as a result of the many challenges that arise when having to care for a physical body, and it didn't take long until competition for scarce resources turned others into a threat. Life was difficult and tinged with sadness at the loss of the carefree existence they had left behind. Many regretted their decision, but at that point it was too late to return to Source at will. They were truly lost. For a very long time, humans remembered their origins, but the memories became ever more distant, and finally there was total amnesia.

'This is our creation myth in a nutshell, except that it isn't a myth. Naturally, there is more to it. Designing the human body with all its organs and physical senses, along with its psyche that was to contain thought, emotion and memory, and fine-tuning it all so that it would be able to survive on the planet, was a highly complex, elaborate process. It took place over an unimaginably long period of time, but this is essentially what happened.

'Gradually, human beings became better at living on Earth – they had been a bit clumsy in the beginning – and many started to enjoy the process of creative manifestation in the physical world. However, there was always an underlying sense that something was lacking. Your feeling, my friend, that "there must be more to life", which you felt over so many lifetimes, was caused by a vague memory of all of this. It was a sign that you harboured a deep desire to go home. When you were passing through this place of near-mythical perfection, which we called the Garden of Plenty, you were, on an unconscious level, reminded of the paradise-like quality of Oneness. But rather than recognising it as such, you acted upon the deeply felt, primordial pain it triggered, the grief for what was lost, and this was what spurred you to look for these qualities of perfection somewhere else. You came very close to remembering that time.

'In your present life, when the Master asked you to find the stone, he meant for you to find the way back to Oneness. He wanted you to realise that, even though it seems you are a separate being, you are in fact an integral part of something much larger. His way of doing this was to make you look for a stone that would be the ultimate stone for you, a stone in which you would recognise yourself. The type of stone he asked you to find is known for its healing potential, and there are relatively many of them in that area. When you carry it on your body for some time and the soul-desire is there, it can help you find the path to your innermost being. I think the fact that you held it close to you for ten days and spent so much time contemplating its beauty also contributed to your transformation. These blue stones come from a large rock, firmly embedded in the mountains in that region. Over time, through Earth's inner stirrings, bits of stone broke off from the big rock, and were strewn on the surface of the Earth. Like this, they became separate stones, but each still carried all the characteristics of the original rock from which it had broken away. Every bit of stone that split away from the whole is unique, no two are exactly the same. You would know that better than anyone, as so many have passed through your hands. You have seen the countless shapes and shades of blue through which this kind of stone expresses. Big or small, smooth, angular, opaque or sometimes almost transparent, deeper or lighter in colour, shiny or dull … so many individual appearances. What they have in common is that they once were connected, forming a seamless whole, a very long time before they gradually started breaking away from the big rock. It's up to each individual stone to remember that once it was part of that massive rock, and to start sensing again that all the qualities of that rock are conserved in each and every one of them, even the tiniest chip.

'When you showed the Master the stone, he told you that what you had found was indeed the most magnificent stone in one sense, but that in another it was not, and this confused you. When he said this, he meant that you had found *your* stone. You knew without a shadow of doubt that no other stone would be as close to perfection, that it really was the Most Magnificent Stone the Earth Could Ever Yield and that you had come to the end of your quest. You had found the key to your true being, but you didn't recognise it. Remember those first moments, when you held the stone in your hand? You felt it speaking to you, but you were so excited that you didn't listen long enough to hear its message. The only way for the Master to make you see that you had to look further than the stone itself was by rejecting it. The profound grief this caused challenged everything you had believed in until then, even, momentarily, your love for the Master. Never had you been able to see that the unique Blue Stone that is you carries within it the knowledge of its origin, and that you are a precious part of a much greater whole. This is what the Master wanted you to realise. You may love the Master and respect the Master, but you must understand there is nothing he knows that you don't. The Master himself would be the first to agree. He needed to shock you to the core and strip away everything you loved and believed in, to bring you back to the realisation of who you really are.'

There was a long pause. After a while, I found myself visualising my own Blue Stone. I should find one. Not that I would join an excavation party, but there were shops where you could buy these kinds of stones. Or was I making the same mistake as Jason? Just as he didn't need to go digging for compassion, there was perhaps no reason for me to visit our local New Age shop. Holding the stone in his hands and carrying it close to his body had been the way for the Seeker for Stones. I would have my own way.

Ian opened his eyes and took a sip of water. 'Wasn't that beautiful?' he said. 'I will let them come back, don't worry, but I'd like to be with this moment a little longer myself. In all the years I've been doing this, I've never been entrusted with two such wonderful beings who are so close to the wisdom of the universe while at the same time genuinely open to human emotion. It's such a good reminder that when we live on Earth, we need to be fully grounded in that Earth-experience. Being conscious of a higher perspective is immensely helpful when you are negotiating the ups and downs of life in physicality – that's why you come to these evenings – but these amazing souls are showing us that we should embrace our existence as human beings and the warmth and companionship of others in a way that's only possible in our here and now on planet Earth.'

He nodded thoughtfully, then turned into himself again. 'I think it's the Sage,' he said. 'He would like to come back.'

'Your medium is right about living life on Earth to the full and not spiritualising it too much. You have all of Eternity to be a spirit of some sort or another, or even pure Consciousness, whatever you perceive that to be.' He laughed heartily. 'Only human beings living on Earth have the ability to feel emotion. It's a crucial skill, challenging of course, because emotions can be so painful and all-consuming. But it's the universe's way of communicating with you, and if you can hear the messages, your life will have flow and be joyful. Make the most of it while you can!

'But I wanted to tell you about the Four Portals of the Heart …

In the life we have been speaking about, when I was a Sage, I learnt about the heart from a very young age. I grew up in a village a few days' walk downstream from the hut where the Seeker for Stones found me, where the big forests start. We deeply respected the river, and we worshipped the trees. Some of them were gigantic and had similar qualities to the pine tree in Esin's village. Our relationship with nature played a central role in what we called The Harmony. Children were educated carefully in this tradition, and some were chosen to devote their lives to actively maintaining The Harmony for everyone. I was one of a small group of children, boys and girls, to learn from our village healer, who was a wise man with many talents. We learnt the practical healing arts, to do with herbs and incantations, and he taught us to read the positions of the stars and how these influence our lives. I have treasured memories of our pre-dawn walks during clear nights. He would take us along the river to a large clearing, and there we would sit, observing the sky and listening to the water softly lapping against the bank. He would point out one or two stars, then encourage us to sense them and let them enter us in any way we wanted. It was there that I had my first experience of the Oneness of All Things. As I opened myself to the light that brightly shone down on us, I felt it pouring into my body – there was a subtle tingling all over me – and I knew it was the star's wisdom. From then on, I reminded myself many times a day to be open to whatever might want to impart its knowledge to me – trees, birds, the river and, of course, the hearts and minds of people.

In the daytime, our teacher taught us in front of his hut, where we sat in a circle underneath a roof made of large, strong, shiny leaves that protected us from the sun or the rain. In the rainy season, the sound of the rain on those leaves was magical. It could be ferocious and last for hours, and the intensity and relentlessness of the sound would bring on a kind of trance state. After it stopped, there was a gentle dripping from the trees for a long time afterwards, which would gradually awaken us and bring us back to our normal consciousness. I would like to tell you about a lesson that took place during one such heavy rain.

Before the rain became too loud to make himself heard, our teacher had started talking about what he called our spiritual heart. We all knew what he meant, because it was one of the first things every child in our community was taught. My family, like all other families, would start and end each day with all of us sitting in a circle, one hand placed gently on our chest. We would look each other in the eyes and see The Harmony reflected in the eyes of the others. Perhaps you can imagine how this ritual contributed to our experience of the Oneness. It reminded us of our origin, that everything and everyone has the same beginnings. Even the youngest children were part of this, sitting quietly on someone's lap, touching their hearts with their little hands. Children have an inner blueprint to be just like everyone around them. When they are very young, they learn by imitation and osmosis, which are the most natural ways to learn, the most complete, too. Being included like this gives them a sense of belonging and security and profound joy. At the same time, it prepares them to be well-integrated, responsible members of their group when they grow up.

So, on that day, just before the sound of the rain on our roof became too loud, our teacher asked us to imagine the water splashing on our heart, washing away anything that might be obscuring its deepest knowing. We loved feeling the force of nature and were keen to do what our teacher asked. We sat there for a long time, until the rain became lighter and there was only the sound of drops on the leafy roof. We couldn't wait for the teacher to ask us to share our experiences, something he always did.

'I felt so strong,' one girl said when the teacher pointed at her, 'I felt the strength of nature inside my heart and then in all of my body, and I knew there was nothing I couldn't do.'

'I saw all kinds of lines and shapes,' said one of the youngest boys, 'some had angles, others were kind of roundish ...'

'My heart became like a rock,' another girl said, 'and I knew that it would forever anchor me in its knowing.'

'Thank you,' the teacher said. Then he pointed at me. 'Could you please stand up?' I did as he asked. 'Show them your chest.'

I let my tunic slide off my shoulders a bit to uncover my upper body. When I looked down at my chest, I saw what our teacher had already seen: four luminous arches. Each of them was a little different, but they were all the same size, and together they took up almost all of my small, bony chest. Their soft golden light invited me in, and all I wanted at that moment was to close my eyes and enter through those arches. Everyone was quiet, staring at the arches.

'Thank you,' said the teacher after a while, 'you may sit down again.'

I did so and looked down at the arches once more, just in time to see them fade and disappear. They only disappeared from sight, however, and I felt them there every day, until the end of my life.

He stopped here and we were as quiet and amazed as the children must have been when they saw the arches on the chest of their friend. The golden light of the arches had somehow made me feel strong, like the girl in the story. It was a pivotal moment, as if my heart too had been washed clean by that torrential rain.

'Those arches were The Portals of the Heart,' the Sage then said. 'You could think of it as a spiritual teaching device, a kind of road map, to show you the way when you feel lost and don't know what to do. In actual fact, it is a comprehensive metaphysical framework that has been used by teachers and healers in various forms throughout the history of mankind. When you study it in-depth, with the right guidance, it lets you discover the wisdom of the universe that lies deeply buried in every human heart.

'When I was growing up in that village in the forest, our teacher took many years to show us everything we needed to know about the spiritual heart. He rarely spoke more than a few sentences, and as much as possible he let us explore and discover things for ourselves. Every morning, we would start with practical exercises, which were often like games. We would move about in pairs or little groups, synchronising the movement of our bodies. We also sang together, or just experimented with our voices, feeling the sound reverberating in different parts of our bodies. Hearing and feeling the vibration of our voices reminded us on an unconscious level of the primordial tone of the universe from which everything springs into being. Another reason for these exercises was to make us feel more together as a group and to heighten our sense of trust. But all of that I only saw much later, when I had grown up. Our teacher never tried to influence our experience with his interpretations. We might have been selected at a young age to receive this knowledge, but we were allowed to learn in ways in which children learn best, through all our senses and with a wide-open mind. I truly had a wonderful childhood …'

He smiled and was quiet.

'So … The Portals … yes …,' he finally said, and for a moment it was as if we were talking with a real old man who was distracted by memories and needed a while to come to the point. It was touching and felt completely natural. I thought of what Ian had said a little earlier, about how there seemed to be no discrepancy in our guests' ability to feel emotion as human beings and their profound, other-worldly wisdom. Just then, Ian resumed, and the Sage became a teacher again, even sounding a little stern.

'The Portals of the Heart is a tool to help you see a larger truth about yourself, something which everyone longs for, mostly unconsciously. Recognition of the heart's great potential for healing the human condition is growing in your here and now. Just as well, for these are crucial times for planet Earth and the many souls that have chosen to live on her. This is a period of accelerated learning that is without precedent. Your planet is stirring with all her might to get your attention. You are faced with critical ecological imbalances and ever-increasing inequality, as well as tricky pandemics thrown into the mix every now and again. Maybe you can see how all of this is Earth's way of reflecting the false belief that is separation and where it has led you. Living in physicality at this time can be bewildering, as events are gaining momentum to make you see there is a strong, collectively felt need to radically change direction. The ability to enter your heart, in any way you can, will be crucial in this process.

'The first of the four is the Portal of Compassion, and if it were the only portal you ever enter through, you would be living a life of harmony and contribution. That is why Compassion Personified came to talk to you ahead of us. The second portal is the Portal of Truth, followed by the Portal of Trust. Finally, there is the Portal of Wisdom. You do not need to take them in that order – it depends on the circumstances – and all portals lead to the same place in the end. Often, entering through one and then through another helps you go deeper. The number four stands for the four cornerstones of a structure that is sound and safe and dependable – that is well-supported. "Four" is also reflected in the four elements of Earth, Water, Fire and Air, and we will show you how these relate to the Portals.

'The Portal of Compassion is usually the easiest to access. As it is the bedrock on which all else rests, its element is Earth. When you show others compassion, you assure them of the ground underneath their feet, so they feel supported and safe. You give them a sense of their shared humanity and a moment's respite from the illusion of separation.' I was taken back to that time when Lozeh had given me an experience of 'the ground that connects us all'. Ground … Earth … compassion, of course! I had slipped into the group and into spirituality with ease after that first evening, and had become more relaxed and less inclined to think I always needed to make things happen single-handedly. Help was forthcoming much more often than I used to think. 'Judgment is the biggest obstacle to compassion,' the Sage carried on, 'yet, it is widespread, habitual and often unconscious. When you enter through the Portal of Compassion, you leave all judgment behind. When you stop judging others, you see them as the unique beings they are, which gives you a chance to appreciate a situation through their eyes. Understanding the experiences of others from their viewpoint will expose you to the never-ending variety of personal truths that souls take with them into their human lives.

'Once you have entered your heart through the Portal of Compassion and left all judgment at the gate, it is easier to pass through the Portal of Truth. Its element is Water, for its transparency and formlessness. Some people believe that truth is fixed and unchanging. It gives them something to hold on to, which makes them feel secure. But you cannot hold on to water. The only constant in life on your planet is change, something wise teachers of all times and on all continents have been telling you. So, if you would like to pass through the Portal of Truth, be prepared to be as flexible and adaptable as water. The symbol of this portal is a hexagon. It stems from the numerology of a very early civilisation that equated the energy of the number six with change. Truth has endless facets and we really mean endless. The totality of Truth cannot be seen in your dimension. It is only visible in the dimension of Source – or Unity, Oneness, God ... Please, leave any words that cause resistance at the gate, as well, along with judgment. Resistance causes a heart to close, and then no portal can lead anywhere.

'Let's look at the Portal of Trust now. Whether or not you trust another person or a particular situation has everything to do with how much you are in touch with the intuitive knowing of your heart. Trust is about following life and understanding that there are no what-ifs or should-haves. Its symbol comprises two horizontal lines, one representing the knowing of the heart, the other the soul who follows it. The element is Fire, the spark that connects those lines and gives you the courage to follow whatever your heart tells you. At times, you may be confused and wonder what your direction is. Entering through the Portal of Trust and following what you find becomes easier when you remember the relative nature of truth. It makes you see that any decision your heart takes will lead you to a meaningful experience and can never be wrong. The main obstacle to this portal is the logical mind. It has a habit of infiltrating trust with fearful ideas. It can happen, therefore, that you think you are following your heart but in reality it is the mind trying to lead you astray with its tempting rationalisations. This is a central dilemma for most people. You have to be alert to the mind's tendency to stealthily insert itself into the subtler heart energy of trust. Paradoxically, trust itself is the best way to keep the mind at bay. If you are not sure if it is the mind or the heart that is leading you, enter once more through the Portal of Compassion. It will anchor you more firmly. Then listen again.

'Finally, there is the Portal of Wisdom. Its element is Air, as it can penetrate everywhere. Its energy is subtler than that of the other portals, and, like the oxygen you breathe, it is absolutely vital. Its symbol is a single, one-dimensional point, where all is contained, reminding us of the point of Oneness. It can also be seen as representing the point of entrance to the fullness of potential that is each present moment, the only place where anything real is possible. Entering directly through the Portal of Wisdom is rare, but being anchored in the now will help. Once you have found the way into your heart, you have complete access to all its wisdom, no matter which portal you entered. In the centre lies your Blue Stone, a seamless part of the totality of Divine Consciousness. Here, you will discover that it never left its source, and that, indeed, separation is an illusion.'

THE SAGE

Red threads are unravelled

When the Sage finished talking about the Portals of the Heart, there was no invitation to ask questions. As I was driving home that evening, it struck me that, no matter what the topic, the theme of connection would crop up. 'Red threads,' they had said once. We had seen these threads in the ongoing life-lessons of the protagonists and in the ways in which they kept meeting and supporting each other across lifetimes. There had also been connection in another sense, when our guests responded to our unexpressed thoughts and emotions. I was amazed that they had picked up on my lollipop frustration, for example. Being seen and understood without having to explain was a profound experience. It was the same for Ralph and his exam. I had asked him around for dinner, together with Elspeth and Jason, and we talked about what Compassion Personified had said to him. It had been a real break-through, he told us. He was much more at ease, so different from the Ralph I had known all those years.

I was glad I had followed up on my feeling that we should include him more – it had been really nice to get to know him better. My thoughts went back to the Portals of the Heart, yet another way of connecting: a tool designed to help us relate to the deepest part of ourselves. I couldn't imagine anything more important.

When I came home Colin was asleep. I said a quick goodbye to Charles, made a cup of tea, put another log in the pot-belly and sat at the kitchen table to write down what I remembered. What the Sage had said about the Portals of the Heart was still very much with me. Apparently, all the portals were connected somehow, and all led to my Blue Stone. There was no wrong way. This was essential, I realised – there would never be a reason for anyone to give away their power to someone they might see as wiser, like the people who had followed Sarwhar. Only a few years ago, something like that could have easily happened to me. I had grown in confidence since joining the group, and was sure by now that it was never a good idea to submit to the authority of another person when I could find answers in my own heart. It was the seat of my Blue Stone, wasn't it? Sacred ground, deeply personal, my space to explore and make discoveries. How fantastic to have been shown a way to access that holy place!

Next time I wasn't sure what to do, I would use the Portals … enter through the Portal of Compassion and stop judging myself or blaming others. After that, pass through the Portal of Truth and remember the diversity of truths and that mine has as much validity as anyone else's. That would be a possible route, wouldn't it? Or perhaps, if I felt compassion deeply enough, it would take me straight to my Blue Stone? Actually, this happened at times, now I came to think of it, but those moments were so brief that I would only realise it afterwards. There were always distractions, little dramas and sometimes bigger dramas, and then I would forget all about Oneness or wisdom for a while. I sighed. Understanding what The

Portals were about hadn't been so hard, but making them an integral part of my life surely was another matter. The Sage had learnt about The Portals as a child, when they had appeared on his chest. Would I ever be able to know my heart like he knew his? After a while, my thoughts wandered to the Portal of Trust … when would I need this Portal? When life threw unexpected events at me that forced changes I didn't want? One of those dramas? 'Life is always as it should be,' the Seeker for Stones had said. It sounded easy, but I often struggled with life's plans for me. When I first joined the group, I used to tell myself off for that – resisting life's flow surely wasn't very spiritual. But our visitors had warned us that thinking of ourselves or others as spiritual or unspiritual was insidious and would always lead away from the heart, just like any other judgment. Much better to simply accept that we weren't perfect, and take it from there, ha-ha. Passing through the Portal of Compassion and dropping all judgment would bring awareness of the spiritual nature of all beings, regardless of what they said or did or looked like. I could suddenly see it so clearly.

Again, I marvelled at compassion's power to ground us and bring us back to the basic truth of our shared origin. Compassion Personified had said that he lived inside our hearts and in fact was us. Or that we were him … or her or them. Finding compassion was only a matter of accessing what was right there. How difficult could it be? I sat at the kitchen table with my notebook until late, inventing scenarios and finding possible routes into my heart through different portals. It was fun and fascinating and incredibly empowering.

Because of all of that, I felt I had grown a bit by the following Thursday when I walked through the gate of Magda and John's garden. Before entering the studio, I paused for a moment to listen to the water trickling into the lily pond and greet the Buddhist Madonna. I went inside, sat down next to Jason and waited in silence with the others.

For a while, there had been no quick catch-ups before the sessions, only a whispered greeting. Not that it had become gloomy or overly serious; it was more that we had come to appreciate the power of silence. Ian was late. I suspected it was his way to contribute to our silence-learning. When he came in, he greeted us warmly, and a few minutes later the Sage was there again.

'Good evening, I am so pleased to have a chance to talk to you once more. I am the one you know as the Sage, even though that was only one of the forms through which my soul expressed Consciousness on Earth. "The Sage" will do for now. I would like to tell you about two of my other lives, so you can see how beautifully everything fits together. The people you feel closest to in your present life are almost certainly beings with whom you share a soul history. These kinds of connections are based on fundamental love bonds, and there is a natural pull to continue and deepen that love.

'My very dear friend the Seeker for Stones mentioned that my visits to planet Earth were less for my own good than that of others. This might be true in some ways, but please don't think this makes me a better kind of soul. The pocket of consciousness that is my soul never ventured out as far from Source as some others did. In some ways, you could say that I played it safe, or that I was lacking a sense of adventure and curiosity. I don't consider myself a coward because of that, but nor am I a superior being. The Seeker for Stones was much more adventurous and went deep into the human experience. I have followed his many lives with admiration and learnt a lot from him, from the depth of his emotion and his resilience in the face of loss, as he kept searching for life's meaning. The courage to feel, and feel deeply, is something I will never have quite like him. I decided to support him until he found what he was looking for. It was one of the reasons I came as Baddar, the baby who was born at such an inopportune moment, or, at least, that was what it looked like at the time. You have already heard how that birth affected the lives of Nila and Sarwhar, but there was someone else in the mix, someone who mattered even more to me then. I mean my mother, Andisha.

'Andisha had been my mother once before. Our main aim in that earlier life, hers and mine, had been to help the soul that was my father, who was grappling with a persistent false belief – that every human being was intrinsically evil. I am sure you remember the story. I was called Navīd and was brought up by my father and aunts, because my mother had not survived my birth. From a human perspective, not being able to bring me up herself could be seen as a cruel fate. However, it was what she wanted. We understand this might feel like a terrible sacrifice to you, but once you are ready to be of service in this way, it isn't like that. The picture is so much bigger then, and you are simply happy to be part of a large, wise team, steering another being towards an outcome that is desired by all involved. So, please don't worry, and rest assured that these actions always come from free will. No one is ever pressured.

'Much later in that life, my father did come to accept my dream. When he realised his son had been right and had done his father a great service, he was distressed. He felt deep regret that he hadn't been able to act upon that brief moment of clarity, when he was afforded a glimpse of the truth that lay deeply buried in his heart, and instead had sent me away. In that life, we never met again. Sometimes, it is through the kind of sorrow my father had to endure that we gain insight. Emotional pain emphasises the message in a way that eventually helps resolve the issue. The universe has no intention to hurt, and when these kinds of life-lessons take place, it is invariably only after many gentler reminders and opportunities that weren't recognised as such. Unfortunately, it cannot be different – yet. Once you look back on a life, you see your experiences from a different angle, and then you understand. When we all met again, myself as Navīd, my father, my mother, who had left me at birth, and the soul you have met as Ardashir, the healer, we celebrated. First of all, because we were reunited and free to love one another without the restrictions of soul agendas. And also because my father now knew once and for all that people are divine beings and inherently good. This meant that, much later, he could take roles in which he guided others in this respect. It's what makes a good guide – the very high level of empathy that comes from personal experience.

'But I wanted to tell you about that time when I was Baddar and Andisha my mother. Because she had volunteered to go back to Spirit when she gave birth to me as Navīd, I wanted to thank and honour her this time and give her an experience of totally fulfilled motherhood. The timing of my birth was the beginning. The love of a mother for her child is sacred. It is the closest connection possible between two people, beginning, as it does, in a symbiotic way that mirrors the original Oneness. My mother, Andisha, knew this intuitively, and she had bonded with her baby when he drank from her for the first time, only moments after his birth. She and I were very close. She always knew what I needed, long before I could speak, and when I was older we often laughed together about little things no one else seemed to even notice.

'When I was about two weeks old, we left the settlement where we had found hospitality after our journey with Sarwhar had come to such an abrupt halt, and we started the long trek towards the east, away from the desert, with me snugly tied to my mother's back. We detoured a bit to accompany Nila and Gulrang to the settlement of Nila's family, then continued our way to the village where my father and his brother had come from. This is where we settled. The family of my father and uncle were thrilled to see them back after so many years, and they were delighted to meet their beautiful new daughter-in-law and sister-in-law, and me, their youngest relative. Their village was right on the coast, at the estuary of the same river on whose banks I was reunited with the Seeker for Stones, although still far from that exact place, as it was a very long river. The sea provided fish in abundance. I grew up with my cousins and other children, playing with them and collecting fine grasses and other plant material, which the women and older girls wove into fishing nets. They sat in small groups, singing, chatting and laughing, while their hands were busy weaving, the youngest children happily crawling around them, sucking on the juiciest of the grass stems. At sunset, we prayed together to Great Unity. I had no brothers or sisters, which contributed to the closeness between me and my mother. Often, the women took us to the beach, where we would collect seaweed and shellfish. The men would fish in the ocean. They had small, stable boats, and when I was older my father would take me along with him and the other men and older boys. It was a very happy and in many ways uneventful life. That is, until the day a tidal wave hit our village. I was twelve years old. It was early in the morning, and we were all in our huts. There was no chance for anyone to get away. We just held each other, my father, Janan, my mother, Andisha, and I.

'Once we were in Spirit, it didn't take us long to remember, and we rejoiced. My mother and I had reconnected, exactly as we had wanted to. She completed an essential life-lesson at the time of my birth, when she came to understand the nature of Great Unity. For me, Baddar, there had been no explicit life-purpose other than the love bond with my mother. These kinds of lives, led purely in service, are the icing on the cake. Dying young isn't seen as a tragedy. I felt it wasn't necessary to go through adolescence and adulthood. I could have decided to live longer – it was entirely my choice – but this was a life to celebrate my mother and the love between us. Going back to Spirit together when I was still a child, before I would need to separate out from her – at least to some extent – as an adult, strongly enhanced this.

'For the soul who was Andisha, that life was the last. I decided to go back to Earth, to learn more about The Portals and to support my friend, whose soul was so intimately related to mine, and who was so close to finding his Blue Stone. As you have seen, it was wonderful to reunite when we finally did. It rarely happens that you live on Earth with as much knowledge of your life purpose as we had during my life as a Sage. We came as close to Oneness as is possible when living in two human bodies. We had two years like that. One evening, I knew the time had come for me to leave. He knew it as well, and before we went to sleep, we embraced. There was no sadness, only gratitude. We had accomplished what we had set out to do and were certain we would meet again and continue our work in another realm. Not long after I had left the planet, word got around that there was a "new Sage", and soon many came to see him and seek his counsel. Later, when he joined me in Spirit, we had a lot to talk about, a bit like you when you have a good catch-up with your best friend after a long holiday.

'He went back to Earth once more to guide others to the portals of their hearts. Then, he decided he wanted to have one last life to experience simple happiness. He would not chase after Truth nor would he be a Wise Man, and he designed a life accordingly. He was born on a small farm to older, first-time parents, who had almost given up hope of ever having a child. They were overjoyed when he was born and loved him with all their hearts. After their deaths, he stayed on the farm and married a girl he had fallen in love with when he was sixteen. Together, they had three children, who all helped on the farm. A few times a year, the family travelled to the market in town. Other than that, they stayed at their farm and looked after their land and animals. Everything was healthy and well cared-for, and they took pride in all of it. He rejoiced in his grandchildren, who lived with their parents on the farm. He had no knowledge of any particular teachings, and, of course, there was complete amnesia about his other lives. Only when I came early one morning, when he was still fast asleep – he was seventy-eight years old then – and told him that it was time to leave his body behind and come with me did he remember, and he was elated.'

He stopped talking and I was glad. Something was bothering me. I was surprised that the Seeker for Stones had chosen such an unremarkable life after being a teacher of the Portals of the Heart. Wouldn't those years as a wise and sought-after 'new Sage' have been an amazing note on which to end his reincarnation cycle? Suddenly, I understood the inadequacy of my ideas of a desirable life, and I saw the extent of my assumptions. I couldn't believe how crude my criteria were and how full of implied judgment. It made me uncomfortable, and I felt an urgent need to think it through. I had never had much to do with 'simple farmers', or even possibly 'simple people', but I felt different about them already. I had always thought of myself as open-minded, and discovering that I had presumed – ever so fleetingly perhaps, but even so – that being a sage must be better than being a farmer was revealing and disappointing. I smiled in spite of myself. This was a time to enter my heart through the Portal of Compassion. At least, I had a tool to address this. I needed to be compassionate with myself first, I knew, and not judge my ideas as primitive or unevolved or elitist or ... my goodness, so many judgments!

'Please don't think this was a typical last life,' said the Sage. 'Nothing typical exists in that sense. There is no need to come back as a farmer on your way to enlightenment.' It felt like friendly teasing, and I knew he had picked up on my unease. I took it as a reminder not to take myself too seriously and relaxed a bit. 'You may choose your last life, any life for that matter, exactly as you wish,' the Sage said. 'My friend wanted to have this experience. You can return to Earth as often as you like. Or much less often, as I liked. You have complete freedom in the matter.' A smile crossed Ian's face. 'Don't worry! Exploration of Consciousness means that you can be creative. Never feel that you should follow in another's footsteps. On this, hopefully liberating, note, I will say goodbye. My friend the Seeker for Stones would like to have another word with you, as well. I will take my leave from you. It has been a pleasure to have these conversations, and I wish you all very well.'

Ian sighed and opened his eyes. Just as well, because I needed a break. The last words of the Sage had reassured me, and I felt better. How amazing that he had once lived on Earth as Navīd! Such a highly evolved soul – that dream about the nature of Good and Evil in one life, and the Portals of the Heart appearing on his chest in another. It was clear that this wasn't a path everyone would walk or even want to walk. I for one couldn't imagine ever having that kind of ambition. At the same time, it was good to know that there was no expectation to emulate the lives of others and no set curriculum. Being given the chance to watch this marathon movie from prime seats was simply incredible, and as we were waiting for Ian to resume, some of the 'actors' went through my mind: Navīd, who was Baddar in another life, and who, in the end, had come as the Sage; Andisha, who had been his mother, twice; Esin, loving and quietly wise, who was the same soul as Nila, and also the beautiful, perceptive wife of the host in the valley. And of course, the Seeker for Stones and his other incarnations of Sarwhar and of the Wanderer who couldn't stay in that gorgeous valley, even though part of him wanted to. I marvelled at the ingenuity of Consciousness.

'Are you ready to continue?' asked Ian.

'Yes, sure, we are, please …' We were all talking at once. He closed his eyes again to allow the soul we had most recently met as the Seeker for Stones to come through.

'Hello to you all, and thank you so much to your medium for letting me speak to you one more time. We have told you almost everything we wanted. I had many other lives and experiences, but there is no need for completeness. It's hard to say where Consciousness will take us in the end, even from my perspective. Our visits to you were intended to inspire and encourage, perhaps provoke a little. I think we managed to do all that.'

He stopped, inspiring Ian to look round the circle. Never before had any of our guests attempted to make eye contact with us in such a manner. Suddenly, I was looking straight into the eyes of the Seeker for Stones, dark and deep-set as we had once heard. They became green, the Wanderer's eyes, matching the jacket his host had given him, then grey, the transparent-grey of the eyes of Sarwhar. I saw them coming into focus and retreating, and, as I was sitting in my chair, hardly breathing, I knew I was witnessing something extraordinary. Mirrors of the soul indeed. After a while, Ian lowered his gaze, closed his eyes again, and the Seeker for Stones continued.

'Before I leave you to contemplate all the red threads, I would like to tell you about those years with the Sage. I want you to know what a wonderful, endlessly wise teacher he was. He was the best role model anyone could ever wish for, and I think you will understand what I mean when I say that I mostly learnt from his being, rather than his teachings, important and beautiful though they were. If I would describe him with only one word, it would be "kind". I would like to tell you about the time I asked him how I could learn to be as kind as he was.

> It was raining that day. We were sitting in the doorway of the hut on two tree stumps that served as stools, sipping hot cinnamon tea and enjoying its sweet aroma while watching the rain that was falling steadily. Fat drops splashed onto the river surface, creating circular ripples that spread outwards, overlapping, separating, and joining again in a captivating display. The river was swollen and much closer to the hut than normal, but not so close that there was a danger of flooding. I enjoyed being so near the water. By then, I was utterly changed. I had loving memories of the man who had dug for blue stones, but the 'I' that I had

become was very different from him. There were still things for me to learn, though – there always are, of course – and as I was sitting with the Sage, immersed in the intriguing spectacle of the circles of water that moved with grace and secret intent, I knew I had to ask him about the kindness that was at the core of his being. His eyes, which were small and deeply nestled in the wrinkles of his finely lined face, started glowing as soon as I asked the question. He playfully ran his fingers through his long grey beard for a bit, and when he started speaking his voice was like the sun, filling the damp hut with light and warmth.

'You are not wasting time. It hasn't taken you long to recognise that kindness is indeed the key.' A large smile appeared on Ian's face, and his head started nodding, slowly but emphatically, and kept doing so for quite some time.

'True guidance is always rooted in kindness,' he carried on when Ian's head was still again. 'You can be nice or friendly and instruct and communicate worthwhile facts and information, even profound knowledge at times, but if you want to help others on their way, you need to be kind. All judgment disappears then, both yours and that of the other. Since you have asked, I will share my thoughts on kindness with you.' He had both his hands wrapped round his tea bowl and took a few careful sips before continuing.

'I have to start with a warning of sorts, which is this: be careful not to fall into the trap of thinking that you should ever tell others what to do. No matter what it is people are going through, it is never about finding a solution for them. Perhaps your solution could provide some temporary relief, but they will always run into the same issue again in one way or another. This is why, when you walked off into those mountains, your guide couldn't do more than he did. Maybe he could have saved you, but it would have been pointless. It was about your process and your decisions, your next step as you created your life-path. Life is creative exploration, and we should never take that away from people by telling them what to do, simply because it isn't kind. We don't want them to worry about pleasing us as the teacher, or about getting it right, which would only increase their fear of failure and undermine their confidence. If we are in a position where others ask for our guidance, we want them to feel completely free to create their lives. Controlled exploration isn't exploration. The kindest thing we can do for someone is respect their life situation, and the best teachers are the ones who make themselves superfluous. If ever a particular life-lesson is needed, life itself will see to that. Never think this might be your responsibility.

'Whenever people came to see me, all I did was enter my heart and, from there, lead them to the portals of their own hearts. Once they find the way in, they start to connect with their inner knowing, which is all anyone ever needs in the end. With empathy, you might have an inkling of what lies in the heart of someone else, but be mindful that it's never possible to have a full picture. Just be kind. Always remember that, even though all Blue Stones originate from the same rock, they are all different. You can only be of service to another human being when you respect their uniqueness.'

He paused, and for a while he gave his full attention to the play of the ripples and the specks of light reflected on the surface of the dark water. I poured some more tea into our bowls and waited until he was ready to continue.

'All of this made me realise that in every encounter between two human beings, each has something to show the other,' he said then. 'Seeing this takes you through the Portal of Wisdom. If ever you reach a point where you feel that other people have nothing to give or nothing of interest to tell you, be still and contemplate. It is a sign you are suffering from the biggest blind spot of all, the illusion of separation in one of its most undiluted forms. There is always a chance for this to happen. As long as you are a human being, you are not exempt. To nurse yourself back to spiritual health, enter your Portal of Compassion, and stay in your heart for as long as you need. Take your time. Then, slowly find your way through the other portals. You might find that your mind was interfering with your ability to trust the knowing of others, or that you forgot that someone else's truth could give you a new perspective. Always be prepared to learn from whoever happens to cross your path, no matter who they are or where they come from. Even as a Sage, I have stumbled upon profound truths through the people who came to see me. They would tell me exactly what I needed to hear, often when I least expected it, and, mostly, they had no idea that this was what they were doing.'

'I was so glad I had asked him about kindness. His answer, along with the light and warmth his words conjured up when he told me all of this, stayed with me during all the years I worked in his hut with people who trusted me with their sometimes harrowing dilemmas or deep despair. He was a living example of what it means to be humble, and I came to understand that true humility never implies lacking respect for yourself. The Sage was always aware of his humanness and was comfortable with it. He was in touch with his own needs as a human being even as he was attending to the needs of others – he never forgot that he was one of them.

'Of everything he taught me, this was the most significant. And the Portals of the Heart of course. I learnt to appreciate more and more how far-reaching this deceptively simple system is, and how empowering. There is a lot to it, much more than the Sage could tell you on that one evening. It took me nearly two years to fathom its depth and rich complexity.

'After those two years, the Sage told me that I was ready to see others, and when he had returned to Spirit, people started to find their way to me, asking for my guidance. It was such a privilege to be able to show others the paths to their Blue Stones, rather than digging into mountains to find them myself. As the Sage already mentioned, I continued his work until it was my turn to go back home. By that time, I had an apprentice who had heard about me after passing through Esin's village – just like I had heard about the Sage all those years before. By the way, her son had returned, he told me, bringing with him a wife and two young sons of his own. I have a feeling you might like that snippet of news just before I leave. My apprentice understood compassion, because he was a kind man. It wasn't difficult to teach him the rest. When I had gone he kept doing the work, and for many generations apprentices found their way to the hut by the river, so that they could learn about the Portals of the Heart and continue the teaching.'

He was quiet, giving us a chance to appreciate the lineage of sages that had spread the teaching of the Four Portals of the Heart. Then the Seeker for Stones spoke one last time, to say goodbye to us.

'It was a pleasure and a privilege to have the chance to talk with you. Thank you for your hospitality! I hope that accompanying me for part of my way and witnessing my soul development – from an ambitious Sarwhar to a farmer who simply tended his land and loved his family – has provided you with insights that will be useful on your own paths. Travel lightly, and enjoy the scenery!'

EPILOGUE

We hear how everyone lives happily ever after

About a year after our conversations with the Sage and the Seeker for Stones, I got a call from Fred, who told me that his firm was relocating him to a city on the other side of the country. There had been talk of relocation before, but he had always managed to persuade the board to let him stay, citing the fact that he had a young son who was living with his ex-wife in the same town. This time, however, there appeared to be no room for negotiation, and he wanted to discuss with me how we could create the best possible situation for Colin.

At first, I felt defeated and was tempted to tell him to find another job, but I knew that in Fred's line of work this wasn't really an option. All of the things I loved about living there went through my mind. I felt very settled and had developed a substantial network. I loved my house and had recently renovated the kitchen. I finally had the perfect set-up to develop a range of foodstuffs and supply them to the stores that had expressed interest after the publication of my second cookbook. And then there were the Thursday evening meetings with Ian. Without a doubt, leaving those behind would be the most difficult of all. At the same time, I wanted Colin to be close to his father and continue seeing him whenever he felt like it, rather than only in the school holidays. Colin loved his father, and it had been hard for him when Fred and I split up. I didn't want him to go through a similar crisis on the brink of adolescence. I said to Fred I wanted some time to think about it, but in the end it was hardly a decision. It was clear that Fred had no choice this time. There was no need to consciously enter the portals of my heart to find trust or wisdom. All I needed to enter at that moment was my mother-heart. So I said to Fred that Colin and I would move.

It was difficult, but only for a while, and I never regretted it. I found a house for Colin and me that felt just right, and had the kitchen extended. Fred contributed a substantial sum. It was his way of thanking me for uprooting my life for his and Colin's sake. He understood that it was a big thing for me, and being able to be close to his son meant a lot to him. It marked the start of a new stage in our relationship, and we became good friends. I launched my product range, Al Fresco with Nicola, about a year later, and published a new cookbook every two or three years for a long time. I kept in touch with Sonia and Elspeth, who were to be friends for life.

Not long after the Sage had told us about the Portals, Ian went through a period of intense, vision-like dreams. He began recording himself in trance and received many new details about the Portals of the Heart, which resulted in the publication of a book of the same name. It was suggested that, in another incarnation, Ian had been one of those sages who had continued to disseminate the teachings of the Portals until long after the events we had heard about. It sounded rather fantastical, and for a while I wasn't quite sure what to do with

EPILOGUE

this revelation, but in the end I saw that it made perfect sense. The intriguing events that shape Eternity don't take place only in ancient, far-away cultures or the lives of wise men. Our twenty-first century isn't exempt from the Space of Time, which is forever stirring and shuffling events and experiences in ways that make us see what we need to see. I thought of that afternoon when Ian and I had admired the liquid amber trees in the park and talked about his mediumship, and I realised he now had an answer to his question of 'Why me?'.

The book was enormously successful, and it wasn't long before he was inundated with so many requests for sessions and talks that he didn't know what to do. This was when Magda and John stepped in. Magda had a background in advertising, and John had been looking for something meaningful to do since his recent retirement. They suggested Ian let them organise workshops for him, and he gratefully accepted. Their garden studio was far too small to accommodate all the people who were interested, and soon they were hiring large venues.

For me personally this was a wonderful development, because it meant that I could stay in touch with Ian and the wisdom he channelled. The workshops were held all over the country, and as often as I could I took weekend trips to meet up with him. Ian had asked Magda to run classes based on the exercises the Sage had told us about – they had been detailed in the book. Her lifelong interest in yoga made her ideally suited for this, and she was thrilled. During the workshops, people could sign up with her for classes in voice and body work based on what the Sage had learnt as a child in the forest. I liked her classes, which were about sensing the energy in and around our bodies and learning to move it. Afterwards, there would be lightness in my body and clarity in my mind, and I would feel more attuned to the people around me. Ian was always glad to see someone who had been part of his 'foundation group', as he called us fondly. He told me he had approached this new development with some trepidation and complete willingness at the same time. Discovering that he had already been a Teacher of The Portals had strengthened his confidence and deepened his sense of connection with his role. He knew that his contribution in life lay, once again, in sharing this wisdom, which felt surprisingly contemporary.

During the years I attended Ian's workshops, I came to a deeper understanding of the nature of truth and trust and, above all, compassion. I'm not sure about wisdom – an occasional by-product maybe. I don't think I'll ever be a Wise Woman, at least not in this life, but there's no need for that, of course. Eventually, I would see that embracing the knowing of my heart and trusting it to guide me, regardless of other people's ideas of what I should or shouldn't be doing, was the main lesson I had taken into life this time round. Just like Nila – and many others. Discovering that uniquely personal, creative power must be one of the most important subjects on our earthly timetable. At a time when we are finding ourselves at a global crossroads and old securities are being pulled out from under us, the ability to enter the heart and feel humanity's intrinsic connectedness could make a decisive difference. Let's hope that many people will have a chance to find their Blue Stones. I am grateful my path crossed Sonia's that day at the gym, all those years ago. Through her, I met Ian, and through him I found the Sage and all those other courageous spirit-beings.

Ian knows that in order to do justice to the teachings of the Portals, he needs to be in good shape, so he has never stopped getting his hands dirty, as he had once told me. He is in his eighties now, but every now and again he is invited to speak somewhere and always attracts large audiences. He is still caring for the trees in his own garden and in Magda and John's courtyard. Because the weeping maples didn't have enough room where they were, he dug them up and turned them into bonsai. He was introduced to a fellow-octogenarian who had been tending and shaping these dwarfed trees all of his life. Ian was delighted to learn a new skill and now has a gorgeous bonsai collection on the terrace in front of his living room.

Colin had a happy childhood with unlimited access to each of his parents. When he was eighteen, he went to university to study marine biology. There he met Emma, and they now have two daughters. They live close to me, and I started making apple muffins with the girls before they were two years old. The eldest, who is six now, has a real flair for cooking. I gave her a pink-and-green striped notebook to write down her own recipes. The first entry was for vegetable soup, made of store-bought stock with baby potatoes, carrots, celery and particular herbs. 'Celia's vegetable soup,' she wrote in big crooked letters all over the page. Every Saturday afternoon Colin drops his daughters off, and they tell me what they want to cook. They are wonderfully free and creative, and with a little bit of help they almost always produce something they find utterly delicious. I simply adore them, and the afternoons spent with them are some of the best parts of my life.

Just before I moved away, I invited the Thursday group for dinner. I prepared one of my most popular dishes, Portobello mushrooms in a balsamic cream sauce, served on a bed of saffron rice. Others brought salads and cakes, making it a true feast. As a farewell present, the group gave me a pendant. It was a deep-blue, circular lapis lazuli.

So, in the end, I had my own Blue Stone after all.

ACKNOWLEDGEMENTS

Heartfelt thanks to

Shamir, with whom it all began, for his wisdom and compassion

Lisa Greenwood, who lent him her voice, for her invaluable input, and for her friendship

Wyoming Paul, for precious moments of inspiration and help at critical points along the way

Maureen Lee, for empathic, meticulous editing

Bente Visser, for inspired ideas for cover design

Wordzworth Design and Publishing, for making this book a reality

ABOUT THE AUTHOR

Karen Lavie is a music educator-turned life coach. Originally from the Netherlands, she is now based in Auckland, New Zealand. *The Blue Stone* reflects her life-long interest in spirituality and metaphysics.

www.ingramcontent.com/pod-product-compliance
Lightning Source LLC
Chambersburg PA
CBHW032117090426
42743CB00007B/379